AMERICA GONE WILD!

Other Books by Ted Rall

Waking Up in America

All the Rules Have Changed

My War with Brian

Revenge of the Latchkey Kids

Search and Destroy

2024

To Afghanistan and Back

Gas War

Generalissimo El Busho

Wake Up, You're Liberal

Silk Road to Ruin

AMERICA GONE WILD!

CARTOONS BY
TED RALL

**Andrews McMeel
Publishing, LLC**

Kansas City

Ted Rall is distributed internationally by Universal Press Syndicate.

America Gone Wild copyright © 2006 by Ted Rall. All rights reserved. Printed in China.
No part of this book may be used or reproduced in any manner whatsoever without written
permission except in the case of reprints in the context of reviews. For information, write
Andrews McMeel Publishing, LLC, an Andrews McMeel Universal company, 4520 Main Street,
Kansas City, Missouri 64111.

06 07 08 09 10 WKT 10 9 8 7 6 5 4 3 2 1

ISBN-13: 978-0-7407-6045-7
ISBN-10: 0-7407-6045-9

Library of Congress Control Number: 2006924331

www.andrewsmcmeel.com

Various cartoons in this collection have appeared in or been commissioned for non-syndication
publication in the *Charleston City Paper*, *Gear* magazine, *MAD* magazine, *Men's Health*
magazine, or the *Village Voice*. These cartoons, as well as those distributed through Universal
Press Syndicate, are © 2006 Ted Rall, All Rights Reserved.

Ted Rall Online: www.rall.com

Thanks to: Jon Bresman, Bärd Edlund, Erin Friedrich, Bob Guccione Jr., Mark Hewko, Ted
Keller, Jon Landman, Paul Levenson, John McMeel, Toni Mendez, Judy Rall, Yvonne Rall,
Sue Roush, Lee Salem, Cole Smithey, and John Vivona.

Foreword

America gave the world the political newspaper cartoon as we know it. It didn't invent it, but took it seriously enough to use it properly. Thomas Nast took a feeble, rather exhausted medium and gave it some real clout. Not for him the Olympian detachment and disdain of, for instance, *Punch*'s Sir John Tenniel. Nast used the medium as the offensive weapon it is most suited to be and made it truly political. He even got results, as Boss Tweed would have confirmed. America also gave us the four-frame newspaper strip and the comic book in all its finery, which is why it is particularly galling to see the way that glorious tradition of fearlessness and savagery has been tamed, not just by commercial restraints and the overwhelming desire of the syndicates and publishers not to offend elements of the readership, but also by a form of latter-day McCarthyism, where an opinion cannot be expressed unless it is "balanced" by an assertion to the contrary, no matter how deranged, and where "fact checkers" bear down on the tiniest details yet ignore the most egregious lies.

The very biggest lies of all are the ones concerning imagery. Why, as we are so often told, is the "Arab Street" or the "Muslim World" in a constant state of outrage with the "West"? Could it have anything to do with the stark and horrific imagery of the factual results of a variety of military actions on a variety of civilians by the Coalition of the Willing in various countries presented daily by the likes of Al-Jazeera? Would such vileness be allowed to be shown in the UK or the USA? Of course not, because that would be considered to be in poor taste. The truth has an unfortunate habit of being in the worst possible taste. That's why Vietnam was a one-off. Don't show the public what wars do because it tends to make them unpopular. And didn't the military learn that lesson well? The ones at the top did, certainly. The ones at the bottom, if they're lucky, go home and try to forget about it. The unlucky ones don't come back at all.

So in these image-driven times, shouldn't the political cartoonist come into his or her own? Isn't there a place for the purest form of visual intelligence in the middle of this torrent of horror, lies, drivel, and pure fantasy? The Chicago-based Tribune Company doesn't think so, since they just got rid of all theirs. A cartoonist is not seen as being anything worth sustaining, and so the product gets blander and more conformist and then they wonder why fewer and fewer people read newspapers.

But it's not all bad. The US of A still has some of the very finest practitioners of this most ignoble yet magnificent art form beavering away in new forms and hitherto unimagined media. The one you hold in your hands is a case in point. He's got a punchy, two-syllable name ending in double L, he's not attached to any one particular paper, and, most important of all yet most unlikely for a syndicated cartoonist, he doesn't seem to be at all bothered by who he offends. Some say he's bugged by the CIA, some say that he's employed by the CIA. That's what I call true "balance."

I'd like to put in a word for us foreign cartoonists. America voted George W. Bush in, but we all have to live with the consequences, and we're not even allowed the chance to kick him out after four years, which America conspicuously failed to take. All we can do is attack the stumblebum chimp fratboy from afar, which lends a certain perspective but has all the impact of a fart in a hurricane. There is one small advantage, though, in that I don't have to live in the same country as the assortment of nutbags who e-mail me their heartfelt threatening history lessons, usually around the general theme of "We saved your ass in two world wars, limey faggot."

This is why I don't envy that arrogant, fluent French–speaking young upstart Ted Rall. Here in Europe we know that every American citizen is obliged to carry a gun over the age of ten, so the idea of trashing your president and your very way of life without having the Atlantic Ocean to hide behind is quite daunting to say the least. So hats off to Rall, who not only outrages sensibilities three times a week in pictures but also lets off a syndicated rant column once a week to boot.

It's difficult to introduce a book from the wrong side of an ocean when your idea of its contents is sketchy and you've only just found out it's to be called *America Gone Wild.* Isn't America wild enough already? I'm sure it'll get wilder when it catches sight of the venomous trash between these covers. I once heard Rall's drawing style described as looking as if it had been carved into his own leg. Indeed, Generalissimo El Busho does seem to have exceptionally sharp teeth, but I suppose, as with all the best cartoons, that this is only a proper reflection of a deeper truth.

Ted Rall is rude, but America needs rude. The last remaining superpower on earth in the middle of a frenzy of outward-bound jingoism needs more than rude. It doesn't just need its flags burned, it needs them shoved up its arse along with "freedom fries," Humvees, shock jocks, lifestyle journalism, and prayer breakfasts. Only in a nation led by a chimpanzee could the theory of evolution be under attack. And they said the age of irony was dead after 9/11! We must stand up for more than free expression. We must stand up for the right to take the piss and to willfully offend the offensive. In a spirit of casual profanity we hold these truths to be self-evident.

Steve Bell

Somewhere in England

Steve Bell is the editorial cartoonist for *The Guardian*.

Preface

Including a Behind-the-Scenes Look at My Most Controversial Cartoons

"Ted Rall of Universal Press Syndicate is arguably the most controversial cartoonist in America."
—Cartoon.com

I produce about two hundred cartoons each year, the vast majority of which are enjoyed, or not, by millions of readers without ever becoming the topic of a news story or talk-radio rant. The closest most of them come to achieving immortality is being cut out of a newspaper and tacked up to an office cubicle, forwarded around the Internet, or reproduced in a collection of cartoons like the one you now hold in your hands. Controversy is exceptional, yet it comes with the territory when you're a political cartoonist. This essay explains how some of my most controversial cartoons of recent years came to pass, how and why they elicited the reactions they did, and how I reacted to the outrage of readers and pundits.

Editorial cartoonists are in the business of producing spiteful parodies of opinions espoused by millions of their fellow citizens. A truly successful cartoon can only be created by including the snottiest put-downs they can think of. An opinion column may contain slanderous bile, as may an illustrated caricature. (See Ann Coulter or Steve Brodner for details.) But editorial cartoons go much further than columns and caricatures, deploying a double-barreled blast of words and pictures in order to expose their targets as unfeeling, murderous hypocrites or much, much worse. Add combustible and divisive politics to the mix, and it doesn't take much for a cartoon to drive usually sane people batty.

Because cartooning is a deceptively simple-looking medium, one that students carry home from school scrawled on the covers of their spiral-bound notebooks, many people think of them as being "just for kids." This secret-weapon aspect of cartooning increases its potency in the ongoing war between differing visions of what is right or wrong. One can hardly blame a cartoon's victims, or their supporters, for taking offense.

Like most of my peers (though, to be sure, there are exceptions), I don't set out to make people angry when I draw a cartoon. Daryl Cagle, a fellow editorial cartoonist who runs a Web site compendium of political cartoons, asserts that I "seem to have a business plan where [I] draw a controversial cartoon every so often so that [I] can get on TV and have Sean Hannity yell at [me]." John Leo, the conservative pundit, claims "[Rall] positions himself as a sort of Howard Stern of cartoons." Trust me, it ain't true.

My goals are to make people think about an issue in a new way and to draw attention to stories that don't receive the coverage that I feel they deserve. Sometimes I'm just out to make my readers laugh. Nothing is more frustrating than drawing a piece whose objective is purely to be funny and longtime readers scan the thing in search of deeper meaning that just isn't there. Other cartoons exist to make you wince. (Unfortunately, some people *laugh* at these.) Each cartoonist has one or more specialties. Although I try to deploy various approaches to the craft, I seem to have a knack for dark humor using images or phrases that make you laugh despite inherently tragic subject matter.

When pundits call cartoonists like me "controversial," their implication is that we political artists sit at our drafting tables cackling with glee as we drool over the piles of hate mail that will undoubtedly result from our latest attack on some societal sacred cow. Nothing could be further from the truth. I'm controversial because I'm *willing* to make people angry in the pursuit of an important point. But controversy isn't my purpose. Pissing people off is acceptable collateral damage. How could I draw a political cartoon if I worried that it might cause someone offense? It is true that, more often than not, howls of affronted anger tend to confirm in my mind that I was right to draw a cartoon. Curses and death threats reveal their authors for what they are. I don't care when those who advocate torture call me names. Why would I want torture aficionados as fans? As a person who expresses opinions for a living, I'm defined by my enemies. On the other hand, a thoughtful and polite letter that expresses disagreement can be persuasive (see page 42 for my cartoon about the 2004 election), and thus far more devastating than a hateful screed.

I had the honor of meeting Mike Peters, the longtime political cartoonist at my hometown newspaper, the *Dayton Daily News*, when I was a teenager. I asked him about obituary cartoons. When is it acceptable to draw a funny cartoon about a public figure who has died? "Communists and dictators are always funny, even when they die," Peters told me. "Play it straight with everyone else." That unwritten rule has resulted in an endless stream of cartoons depicting the dearly departed arriving at the Pearly Gates, exchanging droll witticisms with Saint Peter, hanging out on clouds, wearing wings, going up to the great White House/movie theater/concert stage in the sky. Such pap rarely costs you your job as a cartoonist, but it hardly seems like a good use of space on an editorial page that, if it were paid advertising, would cost thousands of dollars.

My chat with Mike Peters unwittingly touched upon a raw nerve in the American body politic, one that would draw a hail of abuse upon my work after more than a decade of national and international newspaper and magazine syndication. For the Bush years were different. Taking a cue from the take-no-prisoners style of the men in power at the White House, pundits and citizens alike turned meaner. Before 2000 the standard reaction of an American to a cartoon he didn't like was an angry letter to the editor. Now it's an orchestrated campaign to get the cartoonist censored, fired, and blacklisted.

Back when I first began taking cartooning seriously in the '80s, I had promised myself to throw out all the old rules. Gone would be Democratic donkeys and Republican elephants, ships of state with presidents at the helm sinking in maelstroms labeled "deficit," the conceit that political cartoons should be single-panel, and the big head–little body school of caricature. Along with those canards I tossed out Peters's advice about death, though I could have avoided a lot of trouble by heeding his warning.

"Don't give me flowers after I die," my mom says. "It's too late then. The time to be kind to those you love is when they're alive." She's right. Our habit of praising the dead (except for communists, dictators, and now "terrorists") is bass-ackwards. What's the point of setting aside old wounds and ignoring a person's foibles after she's no longer around to care? Despite my mom's impeccable logic, addressing death without sentimentality with a bloodless, muscular approach in place of the old obituary cartoon format—with no more concern for tradition than I had when drawing pieces about other topics—is asking for trouble. Speaking ill of the dead remains a bugaboo of Western, and American, culture. This became triply true after September 11, 2001.

Disaster on such a grand scale, claiming more than three thousand lives and wiping a whole zip code off the map, would have traumatized people anywhere, even in a nation like Israel or Algeria that has suffered a long history of war and terrorism. Americans, who had remained oblivious to the potential for mass carnage despite the bombings of the World Trade Center in 1993, the federal building in Oklahoma City, and the Atlanta Olympic Games, were propelled by 9/11 into a large-scale case of post-traumatic stress syndrome. Their reactions—rage, paranoia, anger, lashing out at enemies both real and perceived—surpassed anything that the attacks' planners dared to have hoped for.

Hysteria drove people to beat and even shoot fellow Americans who, at first glance, appeared to be Muslims. Balbir Singh Sodhi, a turban-wearing Sikh, was murdered outside his Mesa, Arizona, gas station on 9/15 by a "patriot" who previously said he planned to "kill the ragheads responsible for September 11." Mark Stroman's spree of violence began on 9/15 with the murder of Waqar Hasan of Dallas, a forty-six-year-old Pakistani convenience store owner, followed by Vasudev Patel in Mesquite, Texas. He also blinded a Bangladeshi man. "I did what every American wanted to do after September 11th but didn't have the nerve," he told police.

American flags sprouted across rooftops and lawns. Motorists decked out their SUVs like General Patton's staff car. People were scared. Feeling weak, besieged, and unappreciated—how could the rest of the world do this to us after everything we did for them?—Americans turned to their political leaders for guidance.

The Bush Administration and its allies in the media channeled Americans' rage and feelings of impotence into a war lust that fed into the invasions of Afghanistan and Iraq—attacks that, had anyone stopped to think about it, were strange reactions to an operation carried out by nineteen Saudi and Egyptian hijackers recruited by a group in Egypt, funded by Saudi Arabia, and trained in camps run by Pakistani secret intelligence. Much of the White House's wartime propaganda campaign followed drearily familiar historical patterns: a crackdown on domestic civil liberties in the forms of the USA PATRIOT Act and Bush's executive orders to the National Security Agency to tap Americans' phones and read their e-mail, histrionics about the bravery of our troops who were fighting "terrorists" "over there" to avoid having to fight them here in the United States, mass arrests and detentions of Arab Americans that recalled the Japanese American internment camps of World War II, and the smearing of dissidents and opponents of the war (including decorated veterans of previous conflicts) as cowards and traitors.

There was also a new tactic, one that would have surprised anyone familiar with the American people's almost fanatical optimism: the creation of a post-9/11 death cult. Historically most societies that glorified ultimate sacrifice in the service of cause or country have been those that perceived themselves as desperate and victimized. In the Occupied Territories of Gaza and the West Bank, suicide bombers are lionized as martyrs, their images lovingly recorded on street murals extolling their selfless virtue and assured a place in heaven. During the Troubles in Northern Ireland, guerillas of the Irish Republican Army and their opponents in Protestant militias distributed posters and painted murals in tribute to their fallen in a conflict that seemingly had no end game in sight. Imperial Japan's kamikazes flew into American warships after it became clear that conventional warfare wasn't likely to result in their side's victory.

Pathetic "missing" posters appeared on and after 9/11, printed on behalf of people everyone knew were anything but "missing." These presaged the *New York Times*'s project of individual obituaries for each of the thousands of victims who died that day. Dozens of death notices appeared day after day, as summer gave way to autumn and finally to a winter when, unbeknownst to all but a few dozen Americans, their country was already preparing to invade Iraq. New

Yorkers lay awake during storms trying to discern thunder from the rumble of distant bombs. They winced when planes reappeared in the skies. Everyone had a funeral to attend, sometimes two the same day. Wallowing in grief, endless memorializing, and worshipping the dead without thought for their human foibles were symptoms of a society in crisis.

Conservative commentators noted the absurd futility of radical Islamists who believed they would enjoy the pleasures of seventy-two dark-eyed virgins in the afterlife as their reward for martyring themselves in the service of their ideology. What the right soon realized was that 9/11 had also opened the American mind to the possibility that death, particularly in the service of heroic protection of their fellow citizens, could be its own reward. The United States wasn't shattered or defeated like the Palestinians, but its people felt nearly as helpless. If nineteen guys with box cutters could wreak such havoc (by being willing to kill themselves in the process, natch), would the nation survive an attack by more serious-minded enemies?

September 11, 2001, and the subsequent Global War on Terror (or, as the government's internal memoranda called it, GWOT) led the Bush Administration's political marketers to create numerous death myths, each revolving around the nobility of sacrificing one's life for the United States. Deaths initially deemed meaningless and incomprehensible were instantly transformed into sacrifices of almost purposeful intent. The passengers of the flight that crashed in western Pennsylvania, reported at the time to have rebelled against their captors, were credited with bringing down the plane in time to prevent it from hitting the White House or Capitol—thus sparing George W. Bush and/or members of Congress, most of whom were Republicans. The investment bankers, clerks, and restaurant workers who jumped or burned to death in New York—most of whom were presumably, like the overwhelming majority of New Yorkers, liberal Democrats—were deemed to have given their lives for America and, by extension, the political agenda of the Republican Party. Forgotten was the simple fact that they were just people, people who went to work hoping to come home that evening.

And at first the survivors didn't mind it when politicians used their loved ones to push a partisan agenda. True or false, the politicians had given the lives of their lost sons, daughters, husbands, wives, brothers, sisters, and friends meaning. The victims hadn't died in vain. They had died for America, albeit a specific vision of America that they may or may not have agreed with. It was a lie, and the lie's most pernicious effect was to encourage thousands of young men and women to enlist in the military, supposedly to defend America from the evil men who had murdered their compatriots, only to fight and die just as pointlessly as those who had inspired them.

FDNY 2011

The right-wing press, already angered by my depiction of "Generalissimo El Busho," whom I drew as a monstrous Latin American–style dictator in reference to his electoral illegitimacy, drew a bead on me shortly after 9/11. Most commentators had decided to pull their punches about the disputed 2000 election. The few that hadn't went silent after the attacks, leaving people like me standing alone in opposition to Bush, who then enjoyed a 91 percent approval rating. "That is so September 10th," libertarian television talk-show host Bill Maher snapped at me when I brought up the issue on his show *Politically Incorrect*. (ABC, caving into right-wing pressure groups, later fired Maher for failing to agree with Bush that the 9/11 terrorists were cowardly.)

Time magazine even canceled my cartoons—along with those by Mike Luckowich, Don Asmussen, and Jim Siergey—because, an editor told me, "All jokes about the news are tasteless from now on." September 11th was, I would joke, the day America stopped laughing.

As I rode home on the subway that evening, a police officer covered with gray dust sat across from me, disheveled and crying, sucking down an open liter of vodka. Holy crap, I remember thinking, everything *has* changed. Maybe political partisanship will take a backseat to unity against this new threat. Maybe my career as a cartoonist is over.

A few days later George W. Bush unwittingly restored my optimism, not in America but in my future as a satirist. Incredibly he and his fellow Republicans began making speeches, not to the effect that we needed to pull together as Americans, but saying that they would use the attacks as an excuse to achieve their political goals. Tax cuts, fast-track signing authority for free trade, drilling for oil in the Arctic National Wildlife Refuge, war against whomever they decided—it was all theirs for the taking.

If they hadn't changed, neither would I. I continued drawing cartoons that lampooned Bush just as savagely as I had gone after him before 9/11 and Clinton before 1/20, including one that remarked, "Before September 11th, George W. Bush was a big fat zero, a drunken frat boy who cheated and bullied his way into the presidency."

I knew there would be consequences to criticizing a president with a 91 percent approval rating. The Iraq War–supporting *New Republic* listed me on its "Idiocy Watch." The conservative *National Review* tit-for-tatted one of my anti-Bush cartoons: "To which one can only reply that before September 11th, Ted Rall was a big fat zero, an ignorant, talentless hack with a flair for recycling leftist pieties into snarky cartoons that inspired breakfast-table chuckles among the leftist literati and the granola-munching types. And since September—well, very little has changed."

I don't like granola.

Cartoonists are charged with the task of pointing out when emperors have no clothes. They are also obligated to scoff at ideas with no basis in fact. September 11th was a fact. The way it was spun into a War on Whatever We Feel Like was not. The spin relied on building a web of mythology, starting with the attacks themselves. And myths, whether nationalistic, religious, or political in origin, are natural targets for a cartoonist.

The first 9/11 myth, of course, was that the 343 firefighters who died at the Twin Towers were heroes who "orchestrat[ed] the most successful rescue operation in the history of our nation," in the words of former New York City major Rudolph Giuliani. But as Janet Wilmoth, editor of *Fire Chief* magazine later told Salon.com, "The truth will probably never be known because [the rescue effort] was a such a fiasco." By the time the firefighters began climbing the stairs, both buildings were doomed. Their march up blocked the stairs, trapping office workers who otherwise might have escaped. Even if they had made it to the high floors where the fires raged, there wasn't any water pressure they might have used to put them out. The firefighters died for nothing. Moreover, though it doesn't take anything away from their bravery and sense of duty to say it, they died doing their jobs. The possiblility of death is deemed an acceptable risk by most people who take the job.

These are uncomfortable truths. But uttering uncomfortable truths is what editorial cartoonists do. So when publisher Bob Guccione Jr. and I sat down a half mile north of Ground Zero to discuss the subject of my next cartoon for his men's lifestyle magazine *Gear*, the myth of the firefighters came up quickly.

The true victims of 9/11 having been pulverized into bone and gristle, New York's firehouses remained staffed by skeleton crews of men who hadn't made it to Ground Zero for reasons of geography or scheduling. They were being inundated with expressions of grief: cards, posters, food, flowers, money. It struck me as interesting that an essential public service sector funded by taxpayers would collect donations from the citizenry, so that's what I decided to focus on for *Gear*. I came up with "FDNY 2011"—New York Fire Department 2011, a look at the pampered lives of firefighters ten years hence, based on the (of course, ludicrous) assumption that donations would continue pouring in at the same rate.

As anyone who reads it can plainly discern, my *Gear* cartoon doesn't disparage firefighters. It certainly doesn't insult the fallen—it doesn't mention them. Instead, "FDNY 2011" is an admittedly snotty—and, for me, a fairly lighthearted—extrapolation of a slightly odd phenomenon pushed to its logical, ridiculous conclusion.

Nevertheless, cue outrage.

A big part of the right's reaction stemmed from the timing of my cartoon's publication. Due to the lag time typical of magazines, the cartoon appeared just a week after my first major controversy of the post-9/11 era: my "Terror Widows" cartoon, which sent up the unseemly, greedy, and opportunistic behavior of some survivors of those who died in Washington and New York. Because I drew "FDNY 2011" weeks before "Terror Widows," it appears first in this section about my most controversial cartoons. In the minds of many of those who saw it, unfortunately, "FDNY 2011" seemed to follow "Terror Widows" like a one-two punch of insolence and disrespect for the dead.

NEW YORK CITY FIRE DEPARTMENT 2011

TEN YEARS AFTER THE HORRIFIC ATTACKS THAT TURNED THE FDNY INTO A NATIONAL SYMBOL OF HEROISM, A GRATEFUL COUNTRY CONTINUES TO SEND IN CASH.

THIS CAME IN FROM SOME CANCER PATIENTS.

PUT IT IN THE CORNER. VAULT'S FULL.

NEW YORK FIREFIGHTERS HAVE BECOME THE HIGHEST-PAID CIVIL SERVANTS IN THE WORLD. THEIR LIFESTYLES CAN ONLY BE COMPARED TO THOSE OF THIRD-WORLD DICTATORS.

YOU HAVE **33** WIVES AND **140** CARS? HOW DO YOU DO IT?

THIS ISN'T ABOUT ME, MAN. WE'RE JUST DOING OUR JOBS!

Tokyo Exchange +3.125

THEY FIGHT FIRES IN SUMPTUOUS FUR RAIN-COATS. BEST OF ALL, THEY HAVE THEMSELVES DRIVEN TO FIRES— AVOIDING THE OLD DANGERS OF PASSING THROUGH THE WIND-SHIELD IN AN ACCIDENT!

ARE YOU **SURE** THIS IS THE RIGHT ADDRESS, JEFFREY? I DON'T SEE ANY SMOKE.

SORRY, SIR. LOOKS LIKE THE OLD G.P.S. IS ACTING UP AGAIN.

A FEW PERNICIOUS POLITICIANS SUGGEST THAT SOME FDNY LOOT MIGHT BE DIVERTED TO OTHER NEEDS, BUT THEIR EFFORTS ARE ROUNDLY DEFEATED.

SCHOOLS?! IF IT WEREN'T FOR FIREMEN, ALL THE **SCHOOLS** WOULD BURN DOWN!

NO ONE CAN DENY THAT HEROISM DESERVES REWARDS. BUT SOMETIMES, NOW AND THEN, EVEN THE HEROS LONG FOR A SIMPLER PAST.

REMEMBER WHEN WE USED TO PUT OUT FIRES?

SHUT YER YAP! THE SINGA-PORE MARKET'S GONNA OPEN AND I'M LONG ON OCTOBER PUTS!

TED RALL

"The cartoonist who sparked outrage with a swipe at World Trade Center 'terror widows' has a new target—the city's Bravest," reported the *New York Daily News* tabloid. "Ted Rall's latest offering offends too. A new strip by Ted Rall depicts firefighters surrounded by cash, wearing fur coats and riding to fires in limousines. Titled 'New York Fire Department 2011,' in one panel a firefighter tells his comrades sitting amid piles of cash: 'This came in from some cancer patients.' The strip, in the April [2002] edition of *Gear* magazine, has sparked outrage on the FDNY Web site, with angry firefighters calling Rall despicable and writing that he needs 'an old-fashioned ass-kicking.'"

A legal doctrine known as Fair Use allows a newspaper to publish a copyrighted cartoon that is the subject of a news story without asking permission. In any case, Guccione had already agreed to allow media outlets to run it. Possibly because the sight of the actual cartoon would have mitigated the outrage the paper was hoping to stir up, the *Daily News* chose not to do so.

E-mails began pouring in from all over the country. Firefighting-related Web sites had posted the *Daily News* piece, again minus a copy of the cartoon (which also wasn't posted to *Gear*'s stripped-down site should anyone have thought to look). My phone rang. "F**k you, asshole," a gruff voice said before hanging up. How original.

Within a few hours calls were coming in so fast that my voice mailbox was filling up with new messages as quickly as I was listening to and deleting old ones. The firefighters showed up at three o'clock.

Someone was laying on the lobby buzzer to my apartment building, screaming into the speaker so loudly that the distortion made him inaudible, but I got the gist of his communiqué. I looked out the window. A fire engine was parked out front. Roughly twenty beefy men milled about. One looked up. I ducked back inside.

Normally this would have been occasion for joy. What former little boy wouldn't be thrilled to get a visit from a big red fire truck? But in the worst perversion of that fantasy since François Truffaut's film version of *Fahrenheit 451*, the firefighters had come to kick my ass—presumably in an old-fashioned style.

Not knowing what to do and being trapped in my building, I telephoned a pal. "I'll be right over," he said. What could he do against all those brawny men? I called the police (who never appeared) and wedged a chair below the doorknob of my front door and looked for stuff to pile up in the hallway. I'd seen movies.

The firemen left about forty-five minutes later. "F**k you!" I heard one shout. Another Richard Pryor. A polite buzz: my friend. "They're gone," he said. I let him in.

I asked him what had happened.

"I took pictures of them," he smiled, holding up his camera. "Fire engines are for official business, not harassing cartoonists." I considered e-mailing the photos to New York's newspapers but ultimately decided against it. The firefighters' reaction had been unprofessional, but I understood it. They had lashed out at me because they couldn't get even with the people who had killed their colleagues. They would calm down eventually. I didn't want anyone to lose his job over such a lapse of reason.

Postscript: A few sheepish e-mails about "FDNY 2011" have trickled in over the years from firefighters who had later tracked down the April 2002 issue of *Gear*. "I was one of those who yelled at you about your firefighter cartoon," wrote a typical respondent. "Our emotions were still raw after 9/11, which is why the reaction was so extreme. Now that I and many of my brothers have seen your cartoon instead of relying on short news articles about it, we all think it was really funny, in good taste, not at all a slight against firefighters. I've since checked out your other cartoons and have become a fan. I'm sorry for what I said, and please keep up the good work."

Two years later, however, FOX News right-wing attack dog Sean Hannity was still seething about a cartoon most fire-fighters had come to like, or at least had gotten over. This was despite the fact that—perhaps because of it—he had never read the cartoon. "You . . . went after firemen with an ad you had depicting firefighters surrounded by cash wearing fur coats and riding to fires in limousines!" he spat.

"That was a joke," I replied.

"It's not funny," said Hannity, who looked like he was about to spring over the desk and punch my lights out.

"Oh, it *is* funny," I said. "If you actually read it, it is actually very funny."

Terror Widows

My best friend once taught me a useful aphorism. "If something happens once," he said, "it's an incident. When it happens twice, it's a coincidence. When it happens three times, it's a pattern." Since I don't work on staff at a daily newspaper, my work appears days after I draw it. There's no point doing cartoons about today's news because highly topical drawings are stale by the time they appear in print. So I prefer to draw about subjects that seem likely to be in the news for some time. Cartoons about trends—tendencies and phenomena that are likely to continue for the foreseeable future—usually work best.

The "Terror Widows" controversy followed a trajectory familiar to most veterans of media firestorms. First comes shock and an avalanche of criticism. Then your supporters, themselves outraged at the intensity and volume of anger directed against you, issue a counterassault. If you add fuel to the fire, this pattern repeats itself to a more limited extent. Finally people get bored and move on.

"Terror Widows" reflects one peril of my obsessive consumption of news: incorrectly assuming that everyone has seen the same stories I have. I spend most weekdays with the CNN, MSNBC, or FOX News twenty-four-hour cable news stations droning on in the background while I draw. I watch PBS's *NewsHour with Jim Lehrer* every night, as well as the Sunday morning talking-head shows that feature interviews with politicians and government officials. But I don't usually catch the news that most Americans watch when they get home from work at night: the evening news broadcasts of the three major television networks. First of all, they air at the same time as Lehrer's broadcast; second, everything that appears on the big networks is distilled from stories I've already watched in greater depth on cable news.

Trouble is, many of the most interesting stories never make it onto the evening news. I was stunned to learn that the riveting Congressional testimony by survivors of Hurricane Katrina in 2005, who told of New Orleans police who robbed and murdered their fellow citizens in broad daylight—wasn't mentioned on the evening news even though it had been aired by CNN during the afternoon while most people were at work. Had I drawn a cartoon about this genuine news story, everyone would have thought that I had made the whole thing up in order to smear the NOPD.

As the majority of survivors of people who died on 9/11 mourned with quiet dignity, a small but loud subset of opportunists took to the airwaves, using the deaths of their loved ones to promote themselves, their books, or their political and religious agendas.

Barbara Olson, one of a passel of conservative television commentators who appear on the cable news channels, died when her plane, American Airlines Flight 77, was hijacked and crashed into the Pentagon on 9/11. Three days later, one might have expected her husband, Theodore Olson, solicitor general for the Bush Administration and a right-wing zealot who argued *Bush v. Gore* before the United States Supreme Court in 2000, to be overwhelmed with grief and funeral arrangements. If so, one would have been mistaken. Olson, appearing composed and nearly jovial at times, took a break from mourning to shill for Bush's incipient War on Terrorism on CNN's *Larry King Live* on 9/14.

"She wasn't crying, she didn't even sound frightened. She told me her plane was hijacked and that they didn't know she was making a phone call," Ted Olson remembered his wife telling him via cell phone. "What do I tell the pilot to do?"

Olson's performance—his mere *appearance* on television so soon after his wife's gruesome death—gave me the creeps. As it turned out, the Larry King interview presaged a parade of supposedly distraught spouses for whom 9/11 was a mass human sacrifice on behalf of an epic struggle between Christianity and Islam. At the time, however, the Olson interview was a singularity—weird, but hardly worth a cartoon.

Todd Beamer, an account manager for the Oracle Corporation, became famous for, according to an account of his telephone conversation with a GTE Airfone operator before the crash, crying "Let's roll!" before leading a passenger revolt on United Airlines Flight 93, which crashed outside Shanksville, Pennsylvania.

The 9/11 Commission would eventually conclude from an analysis of the plane's voice recorder that the rebellion, if it occurred, did not bring down Flight 93. The passengers never made it into the cockpit. The evidence points to "an explosion of some sort aboard prior to the crash," according to the UK *Independent*. "Letters—Flight 93 was carrying 7,500 pounds of mail to California—and other papers from the plane were found eight miles away from the scene of the crash. A sector of one engine weighing one ton was found 2,000 yards [over a mile] away." We may never know for certain, but Flight 93 may have been shot down by the Air Force.

Like so much of the mythology of the GWOT—the "rescue" of Private Jessica Lynch from Iraqi doctors who had been shot at when they tried to turn her over to American forces; the fictional charge up the mountains of eastern Afghanistan that earned a Silver Star for Corporal Pat Tillman, who was actually killed by fellow Americans—Todd Beamer's "Let's roll" became a catchphrase for a post-9/11 America desperate for heroes. (The 9/11 Commission thinks Beamer's last words were actually "Roll it," referring to an airline food service cart passengers were considering using as a battering ram to gain access to the cockpit.)

Rock star Neil Young wrote a song called "Let's Roll." George W. Bush presented Todd's widow, Lisa, at his 9/20 joint session of Congress. He called "Let's roll" the "new American creed" in his 2002 State of the Union Address. Few Americans know that the Revolt of Flight 93 may never have happened, but it might as well have.

On 9/18, a week after her husband Todd was killed, Lisa turned up on CNN to pimp Jesus. She claimed that Todd had asked the GTE operator "to say the Lord's Prayer with him, and then he asked Jesus to help him. . . . I think he sought wise counsel, certainly in calling on Jesus and saying the Lord's Prayer, and getting his heart right, and I think he also used Lisa in that decision-making process."

As for Todd's death, well, Lisa didn't seem all that bothered: "But, certainly, the faith that I have is like Todd's, and it's helping me understand the bigger picture here and that God's justice will ultimately prevail and that we have more to look forward to than just what we see here around us on earth." If Todd was in a better place, why mourn?

And who had the time? There was loot to be made. Lisa Beamer's "as told to" book *Let's Roll* was announced four months after her husband's death and published in June 2003. Todd, the "hero" of Flight 93, apparently didn't rate his face's appearance on the cover of the book. Lisa, blond and serious and sexy as hell, apparently did. Her publisher claimed that it sold over a million copies, which indicates that it sold at least two hundred thousand.

Then, on February 2, 2002, it was reported that Lisa Beamer had applied for a trademark on the phrase "Let's roll."

"The trademarking of 'Let's roll' is a strictly preventive measure from our standpoint," executive director Doug MacMillan of the Todd M. Beamer Foundation told CNN. "We want to limit its use. We want to be able to protect it, and we want to utilize that to benefit the children."

Beamer's exploitation of her deceased husband to promote born-again Christianity reminded me of Ted Olson's pro-Bush propaganda. Mariane Pearl provided the Terror Widows trifecta.

On January 23, 2002, Daniel Pearl, a *Wall Street Journal* reporter based in Karachi, Pakistan, was kidnapped by Islamic militants presumed to be affiliated with the Al Qaeda terrorist organization. Possibly because Pearl had been investigating attempted "shoe bomber" Richard Reid, a man who had attempted to blow up a passenger jet by lighting his shoe on fire, the Pearl case was tied by the news media to 9/11.

Pearl's wife, Mariane, sat down for an interview with CNN's Ben Wedeman six days later, not to plead for his life—such appearances are recommended by security experts in order to humanize a kidnapping victim in the minds of their abductors—but to describe how difficult the ordeal was for *her*. "It's not easy for me. I'm also pregnant and all these things, and why am I here? Why I'm not, like, not comfortable in Paris." If it occurred to her that her husband might be experiencing a greater degree of discomfort than she could possibly imagine, she didn't say so. Still, it was understandable given her addled state—as was the fact of her appearance.

Unbeknownst to the world and Mariane, Daniel Pearl died on January 29, the same day she was recording her interview in Paris. His kidnappers slit his throat and, on February 21, released a video of his execution.

Just five days after the appearance of the video confirming Pearl's murder, his widow appeared on CNN's *Wolf Blitzer Reports*. Shortly thereafter Pearl appeared on television again to promote two new book deals: *At Home in the World*, a collection of Daniel's essays for the *Wall Street Journal*, and a memoir titled *A Mighty Heart: The Brave Life and*

Death of My Husband, Danny Pearl, that would be optioned for a movie by Brad Pitt and Jennifer Aniston's production company in 2003.

Ted Olson used his dead wife to promote Bush's policies of preemptive warfare and tax cuts. Lisa Beamer used her husband's death to promote born-again Christianity. Mariane Pearl used her dead husband to flog a couple of books. Here, I thought, was an interesting and disturbing trend. First and foremost, what kind of person goes on national television days after their spouse's violent death? Assuming that one has decided to make such an appearance, why didn't they look sad? And if, for whatever reason, they weren't really sad about losing their husband or wife, why couldn't they at least pretend? But I really couldn't get past that first part. What I didn't grasp at the time was that few Americans, especially the Republicans who favor FOX News, had watched the same self-serving television appearances I had.

"Terror Widows," published on February 28, 2002, followed more than six months of unbridled greed at and around Ground Zero. Residents of Battery Park City, a complex of high-rise apartment buildings across the West Side Highway from the destroyed World Trade Center, reported returning to their homes to find them cleaned out—obviously by the police and/or fire departments who had had exclusive access. Shops in intact passageways in the World Trade concourse level had been looted by emergency service workers. Officials of the Red Cross traveled door to door in TriBeCa, one of Manhattan's most expensive neighborhoods, offering $1,500 payments to "victims." Most of these millionaires accepted them.

Finally, there were the widows. Survivors of men who had earned six- and seven-figure incomes complained that the average $1.6 million payouts issued by the victims' compensation fund weren't enough for them to maintain their extravagant lifestyles. Of course, they could have forgone the government's money and sued the airlines for negligence in providing adequate security on 9/11—but whining was easier than fighting corporations through the courts.

One widow told *Time*: "This is a sick joke. I'm ready to throw up," after she was offered a mere $5 million from the fund. It was all a bit much to take for ordinary New Yorkers, most of whom can only aspire to the diminished incomes and $1.6 million checks so many widows were complaining about.

The city was rife with rumors that newly flush 9/11 widows were running off with the husbands of wives unfortunate enough to have husbands still breathing. The *New York Post* confirmed the scuttlebutt on April 14, 2002, when the first widow remarried seven months after 9/11, puffy white dress and all. It was in this mindset that I drew "Terror Widows." Some corrective satire, I felt, was clearly in order. The cartoon's introductory text was designed to show that I was limiting the cartoon's attack to the tiny number of opportunists who used dead spouses for self-promotion, and further to the media's portrayal thereof. The ensuing uproar proves that this text failed to do the job.

The cartoon went online on a Thursday. There was nary a peep from the Vast Right-Wing Conspiracy until late Monday afternoon, when a reporter from the *New York Daily News* called for comment. I was about to become aware of a new phenomenon, the right-wing's so-called war bloggers. Like-minded Bush supporters, fed by official Republican Party talking points and instantly interlinked with a Borg-like hive mind, were able to exercise an outsized level of influence on the mainstream media that belied their small number or qualifications to have their comments taken seriously. Nationally there were fewer than a thousand "major" war blogs, each read by an average of perhaps a dozen people. The ease of laying out professional-looking HTML code online masked the fact that a blog's author might be a twelve-year-old boy or, as in the case of one blogger quoted by the *New York Times*, the dimwitted manager of a telemarketing call center in the Midwest.

Old media editors at the daily newspapers found themselves fielding hundreds of angry e-mails whenever the war blogs urged their readers to express their disapproval. Twenty letters is a high number of letters for a newspaper to receive on a single topic, so editors felt obligated to react, either by issuing an apology or firing the journalist who had caused offense. Of course, the Internet is global—so only a tiny fraction of e-mails coming into the editorial offices of the *Tulsa World* were really from readers living in the Tulsa metro area, and even fewer were actual subscribers. But editors are easily spooked.

"Terror Widows" ran in a number of print newspapers, none of which reported receiving a significant number of negative reactions. It also appeared on the *New York Times* Web site, NYTimes.com, which automatically uploaded all of my cartoons directly from the syndicate since they didn't want to spend money on an online editor to vet Internet content. When the bloggers began harassing the *Times*, the automated aspect of my feature gave them an excuse, first to pull "Terror Widows" from their archives (hello, George Orwell!) and eventually to cancel my cartoons entirely. The *Weekly Standard* (the house organ of neoconservatism founded by Iraq war hawk William Kristol) wrote on March 14, 2002, "Just last week the blogging community took up arms against Ted Rall's despicable 'terror widows' cartoon. A few hours later, the *New York Times* yanked the strip from its site."

As interview requests piled up—"This probably won't convince you but I was a classmate of yours at Columbia," one New Jersey television station reporter said, and he was right, it didn't—I called a fellow editorial cartoonist out west who has been through the ringer numerous times as the result of his hard-hitting cartoons to ask for advice.

"Don't do local television or radio," he counseled. "They'll sandbag you and you won't get anything in return for the abuse. When the Associated Press calls, ask them to e-mail you their questions. Write your response carefully, not off the cuff, and make sure that any single sentence can stand alone without making you look bad even out of context. Newspapers will run an AP quote. You may want to do television, but make sure you address our people—the news junkies who know what's going on. Go on CNN or maybe FOX and make sure they mention your book. At least you should get a few sales out of this."

The *New York Post* ran its story on page two under the headline "*Times*' 9/11 Cartoon Spews All the Views Fit to Offend." The *Daily News* ran theirs on page three. Neither paper printed more than a single panel from the cartoon. There it was again—it's always easier to spark outrage over a cartoon when you describe it. Never let people see it!

"A political cartoon that tries to make fun of terror victims' widows was withdrawn with an apology from the *New York Times*' Web site yesterday—but the unrepentant Manhattan artist offered no regrets," reported the *Post*. "Ted Rall's cartoon, captioned 'Terror Widows,' is aimed at the money relatives of World Trade Center victims are to get from charities and the government—and at what Rall sees as their lack of emotion over their loved ones' deaths."

I followed my media-feeding-frenzy-savvy friend's advice to the letter, and there was only one significant piece of fallout. On March 6, the Associated Press reported, "The *New York Times* pulled the [individual] cartoon from its Web site Tuesday afternoon, when the company received feedback from widows and New York 1, the local TV news channel that broke the story. A spokeswoman for the newspaper, Christine Mohan, said the 'subject matter was inappropriate' and regrets that it ran."

Interesting—the *Times* didn't take issue with my approach or my opinion. For them the entire topic of victims' compensation and questionable behavior by 9/11 survivors was "inappropriate."

"In a statement," continued the AP, "Rall and the syndicate acknowledged the cartoon's sensitive subject matter, but did not apologize. 'Pushing the envelope of polite criticism is what editorial cartoonists do,' the statement said. 'Rall represents a point of view that will not be everyone's opinion. He is looking at a recent news events with the cynical eye of a satirist.'"

I told CNN: "I've done a few lousy cartoons in my time that I'd love to take back, but this isn't one of them." I still feel that way. "Terror Widows" wasn't my best work—I should have referenced the original media whoring that had inspired the cartoon more carefully. Also, failing to identify each character by name made it look like I was going after *all* 9/11 widows—but it was far from my worst. "Terror Widows" helped spark a national conversation on appropriate behavior and avarice from an economically libertarian point of view. Moreover, it helped blow up a cornerstone of Bush's post-9/11 death cult.

Such was life in Bush's America. Regret the pain you've caused and it's taken as a sign of weakness. Refuse to apologize and you're a First Amendment hero. Apologizing to a howling pack of hyenas whose real beef with me was that I was one of the few political cartoonists who had continued to stick it to Bush after 9/11 would have been career suicide. I didn't regret the subject or tone of my cartoon so I didn't apologize. But I did feel bad for the widows and widowers who'd genuinely taken offense.

A. R. Torres penned a rant titled "Wrath of a Terror Widow" for the March 15 issue of the *Salon* online magazine. "Go ahead: Read the hype," wrote Torres, "but don't believe it. Those of us who were wounded to the core by this tragedy are sad and angry and frequently lost. But we are not ungrateful opportunists who have welcomed the death of loved ones as an opportunity to get rich. That person is Ted Rall, and I pity him, more than anything else." My accountant can verify that 9/11 didn't do anything for my bottom line, but Torres's essay was hard to take.

Then I read an earlier Torres piece. Just a few weeks earlier she had ranted about how she felt entitled to receive more and more money for her loss: "I'd like to think that for every flag, there is at least $1 that may come my way. For every word in print, $5; for every sound bite, $500; and for every image, $1 million. In this way, I see the money I receive as royalties from feeding America the sort of media that it desperately needs to consume, day after day. It is the bread under my son's arm, a blighted blessing that feeds us, day after day." No wonder she'd taken offense at the references to money in my cartoon. I felt a little better: the hit dog, as they say down south, barks.

A correspondent to *Salon* agreed: "People die unexpectedly every day," he wrote in response to Torres. "They often leave behind spouses and children who are forced to make do financially, while grappling with their loss emotionally. Can Torres be so self-absorbed that she doesn't grasp this, can't understand why other people might construe 'terror widows' as greedy media hogs? I doubt Rall means to assert that all terror widows and widowers are greedy, media-savvy opportunists, but he's got a strong case that some are. It's not Rall giving 'terror widows' a bad name, but rather people like A. R. Torres, who do court the media. Torres has every right to be offended by Rall's comic, and I can't say that I wouldn't be, given her circumstances. But while many others might simply write a letter to the editor to complain, she published an article on a widely read Web site."

So did another:

Ms. Torres, it seems to me you deliberately and disingenuously misinterpret Rall's cartoon as an attack on the grief of all 9/11 victims' families. Clearly, Rall is making a distinction between ordinary, private, personal grief and the public, gaudy, self-serving, in-your-face variety of some—I repeat *some*—of the 9/11 widows. This latter postmodernist style of grieving (after all, it's a mark of sophistication to make a buck and bolster your ego as you heal, don't you know) is unfortunately becoming all too ubiquitous in Warholian, celebrity-drenched 21st century America, and it's high time that someone stepped up to pillory it. If you want your grief to be sacrosanct and unimpeachable, Ms. Torres, then do not undermine or muddy it with self-promotion, self-aggrandizement, or self-enrichment (I trust you're making a fair piece of dough for your Salon.com pieces) or even the appearance of such. . . . In seeking out public pity (and compensation), you leave yourself open to public criticism. That's how celebrity works, and just because you're grieving as you chase your 15 minutes doesn't mean you get a free pass.

However, the angry right was louder. As usual. Andrew Sullivan, the gay pro-Iraq war blogger renowned for self-interest (he would eventually break with Bush after the latter proposed a constitutional amendment banning gay marriage), wrote: "No paper should ever run Rall again. Censorship? Nah. Decency. And editorial judgment." Sullivan would later talk his way into a "mainstream media" gig at *Time* magazine, presumably using his cries for suppression as a calling card. A blog called Ishbadiddle asked me rhetorically: "Ususally I like your editorial cartoons, even if I don't agree with them. But I just don't understand what drove you to do 'Terror Widows.' What were you thinking? That just because the widows and widowers of the victims of the September 11th attacks are seen as beyond criticism, that you therefore must criticize them?"

That's one reason. And a good one.

On March 11 former Republican presidential candidate and then-MSNBC talk show host Alan Keyes upped the stakes. Keyes wondered aloud whether I should be "punished, arrested? Shot at dawn?"

Whatever happened to turning the page? Calling "Terror Widows" "this brutal and inhuman . . . assault on the decent national sensibilities crucial to the war effort . . . a kind of pornography," Keyes ranted, "Mr. Ted Rall should have been fired immediately by those with professional authority over him, or in contractual relations with him. Such action in defense of the decent judgment of this people in regard to 9/11 would be more than sufficient to keep such as Mr. Rall from subverting our national resolve. But it is worth remembering that when serious and sustained attempts to undermine public opinion on a matter genuinely essential to national life cannot be resisted by other means, *governmental action may be necessary* [emphasis mine]."

Despite a statement of support for free speech issued by the Association of American Editorial Cartoonists, no Republican or conservative commentator or politician disagreed with Keyes's call for government censorship. At this writing I have been unable to locate a single quote by a conservative or Republican opposing the censorship or smearing of opponents to government policies.

Over-the-top commentary dominated conservative radio talk shows and the FOX News shoutfests like *The O'Reilly Factor* and *Hannity & Colmes*. Television chose not to display the cartoon in question, and radio obviously could not. The blogs churned away and my e-mail in-box filled up—my service provider's limit is one thousand. New York police and firefighters called my home to threaten me. "We're going to slit your throat," one cop from Brooklyn—he helpfully left his name and rank with his message, which was verified by Caller ID—yelled into my phone. Who could I call—the police?

My syndicate, having been through far worse when Garry Trudeau's *Doonesbury* had sparked controversy, was as supportive as they could be. But I was, in the end, alone. I asked my building superintendent to let me out down a back alley in case someone was lying in wait at my home's main entrance. I changed my routine, switching from subways to taxis. After about a week, things calmed down. The right-wingers had moved on to their next target. It took months before I stopped turning around to check for stalkers.

The "liberal" *Times* dropped my cartoons entirely in March 2004. By their own admission they had yielded to the demands of conservatives who disagreed with my politics. Daniel Okrent, then the paper's ombudsman, conceded:

> On Tuesday, March 2, cartoonist Ted Rall posted this on his "Rallblog":
>
> "If you read my cartoons at the *New York Times* Web site, you may have noticed a hole on the comics page where my work used to appear. It seems that, under the dismally lame cover of 'moving in a different direction,' my cartoons were the only feature out of 10 (all supplied by Universal Press Syndicate) that the *Times* saw fit to drop."
>
> Rall went on to assert that although he believes a newspaper (or, implicitly, a Web site) has the right to publish what it wishes, he feels that the *Times* has dropped his work from NYTimes.com because "they're annoyed by receiving so many e-mail complaints about my work—all of them motivated by partisan politics."
>
> The *Times*, of course, has a different story. Len Apcar, the editor responsible for NYTimes.com, issued a statement that explained his position. "After two years of monitoring cartoons by Ted Rall," Apcar said in part, "we have decided that, while he often does good work, we found some of his humor was not in keeping with the tone we try to set for our Web site."

Separately, Apcar told me that "I enjoy cartoons and I certainly like to laugh but Ted Rall's work often didn't pass the laugh test. Worse, it was offensive too often."

On principle, I hold with Apcar. Although I happen to think that Rall, while ferociously partisan, can be absolutely brilliant, a lot of his work just doesn't fit in the *Times*'s self-defined environment. But I'm tempted to differ with Apcar's solution. Why not just continue what he and his colleagues have been doing, rejecting Rall cartoons that don't meet *Times* standards? It's worked up until now. Then again, I'm not the one who would have to make the choice every day, and sometimes things like this can just make your head hurt.

What Okrent failed to mention was that the *Times* had frequently run my cartoons, usually one per month or more, in its print edition since 1991 (thirteen rather than "two years"), plus various freelance pieces for the paper's editorial and op-ed pages. In fact, my cartoons had appeared more frequently than any other cartoonist's throughout the '90s. Had my cartoons changed? Or had their "laugh test" become a cover for avoiding hard-hitting work in response to a harsher, more conservative political climate? You be the judge.

The *Nation* editorialized in July: "In light of the struggle for hard-hitting political commentary, Rall's removal from the *New York Times* Web site seems to be another example of the mainstream media's post-9/11 penchant for censorship. It's hard not to be sympathetic to those widows who wrote to the *Times* in their own defense. Their grief cannot be comprehended by most of us, including Rall. But one also cannot stand behind the editors of the *Times*. Whisking away controversial material is no answer."

The *Washington Post* also dropped "Terror Widows" from its Web site's archives.

Postscript: Ted Olson is now a private attorney representing the state of Kansas.

Lisa Beamer has become a regular on the Christianist lecture circuit. For example, she appeared with Dr. James Dobson, leader of the hard-right extremist group Focus on the Family, on November 22, 2002. A 2005 television movie, *The Flight That Fought Back*, featured Bryan Friday in the role of Todd Beamer. A feature film, *United 93*, was released in 2006.

In March 2004 Mariane Pearl returned to the news. First she appealed to Congress to pass a special bill granting her money from the 9/11 Compensation Fund. The fund had rejected her initial application because Daniel did not die on 9/11. "It is getting to the point where [my son is] going to start going to school," Pearl told CNN. "So then, you know, the expenses are going to grow. It's very expensive to raise a kid, you know." Congress refused her appeal.

In April 2005 the *Washington Post*, following up the story of Eason Jordan, a CNN executive who was forced to resign after (truthfully) saying that the United States military had targeted journalists in occupied Afghanistan and Iraq, revealed that Jordan had separated from his wife of sixteen years in order to pursue an affair with Mariane Pearl. She now lives with her son (by Daniel) in a luxury two-bedroom apartment in New York City.

When readers criticized Richard Leiby, the *Post* reporter who broke the Jordan-Pearl relationship story, he replied: "[Mariane Pearl has] been a fairly public figure who hasn't passed up an opportunity to promote herself, her book, and her dead husband's cause. That makes her newsworthy." Bush's popularity was beginning to slip as casualties mounted in Iraq, and Democratic presidential candidates had been emboldened by Howard Dean's insurgent primary campaign based on honest talk about the war. Leiby probably would have been fired or forced to apologize had the same piece appeared in March 2002, the time of my cartoon.

The 9/11 Compensation Fund has been ravaged by scandal and lawsuits filed by widows and other survivors who want more money. Some bloggers have questioned their previous attacks on my cartoon. "Maybe I owe Ted Rall an apology," read a 2004 posting on Random Nuclear Strikes. "So, do we all owe an apology to Ted Rall?" asked a poster to Metafilter. I don't want an apology. I want people to think before joining the next media pile-on they see.

The 2004 Republican National Convention, held in New York as a not-so-subtle attempt to tie the party and Bush to the attacks, included a prime-time parade of 9/11 relatives and spouses who endorsed Bush's reelection campaign. Clearly a "Terror Widows" sequel cartoon was called for to address this tawdry and cynical display of manufactured grief.

There was no significant reaction.

Pat Tillman

Pat Tillman was a NFL football player for the Arizona Cardinals who became famous in 2002 for turning down a three-year, $3.6 million football contract and joining the Army Rangers. Because Tillman's enlistment had been inspired by 9/11, he had hoped to be sent to fight in Afghanistan. Instead the Army first deployed him to the 2003 invasion of Iraq. He was then sent on a second tour of duty to eastern Afghanistan, where he was shot on April 22, 2004. The Pentagon's initial account of his death—that he had died while leading a heroic charge to draw enemy fire away from his comrades in an act that earned him a posthumous Silver Star—was eventually exposed as a fabrication. In fact, Tillman was killed in a tragic "friendly fire" accident.

Tillman's nationally televised memorial service, attended by Arizona Senator John McCain, was a mixture of tribute and war rally. Various Bush Administration officials and Republican pundits lauded Tillman as, in Ann Coulter's words, "virtuous, pure, masculine like only an American male can be." The myth of the rugged football star who passed up a chance to earn millions to give his life in the struggle against Islamic terrorism marked the zenith of the post-9/11 death cult.

As it turned out, Tillman was more complex than either I or Ann Coulter might have guessed. I figured him for a thoughtless, violent jock, a stereotype reinforced in my mind by an account of a vicious fight that landed him in trouble with the law as a young man. Joining the military, I believed then and still do today, was an inappropriate reaction to 9/11. After all, 9/11 wasn't carried out by an army or a country.

In fact, the *San Francisco Chronicle* revealed in September 2005, Tillman was a political progressive who called the Iraq war "so f**king illegal" and "totally was against Bush." He urged his platoon to vote for Democrat John Kerry against Bush in the 2004 election and had arranged a meeting with leftist linguistics professor Noam Chomsky upon his return to America. The real reason he enlisted, his mother told me in June 2004, was because his brother already had signed up. He followed his brother into the service to "watch his back" under a program that allows siblings to serve in the same unit. But I didn't know any of this at the time. ("I don't believe it," gasped Coulter on FOX News's *Hannity & Colmes*. "I don't believe it either," Hannity said.) Like most Americans I bought the official line: Jock joins army to kick Arab butt for Bush. And that's the cartoon I drew.

As with "Terror Widows," I tried to make it clear that the cartoon was less about one man's bad choice than how the media turned tragedy into a heroic example worthy of emulation. That becomes strikingly clear, I think, in the final panel, which depicts how editors spin the events described therein. My complaint was with the media's use of the Tillman story to encourage other young men and women to sacrifice themselves for Bush's illegal and pointless wars, not with Tillman himself.

"Don't you care about Pat Tillman's family?" one interviewer asked me after the controversy broke. "It's too late to care about him," I replied. "If I'd been his friend I would have advised him not to go into the army. Now that he's gone I want what happened to him to stand as a cautionary tale, not an example for young people to follow." Unfortunately, many readers interpreted the cartoon as gratuitous disrespect for the dead.

YOU MAY REMEMBER PAT TILLMAN, THE N.F.L. PRO WHO ENLISTED IN THE ARMY RATHER THAN ACCEPT A $3.6 MILLION FOOTBALL CONTRACT.

ARMY. We're Looking For Guys Who Don't Read the Paper.

NEVER MIND THE FINE PRINT. WILL I GET TO KILL ARABS?

TILLMAN, WHO EARNED $18,000, FALSELY BELIEVED BUSH'S WARS AGAINST IRAQ AND AFGHANISTAN HAD SOMETHING TO DO WITH 9/11.

WE'RE ATTACKING AFGHANISTAN TO GET AL QAEDA, WHICH IS BASED IN PAKISTAN AND FUNDED BY SAUDI ARABIA, AND IRAQ TO GET AL QAEDA, WHICH HATES SADDAM HUSSEIN.

MAKES SENSE.

ACTUALLY, HE WAS A COG IN A LOW-RENT OCCUPATION ARMY THAT SHOT MORE INNOCENT CIVILIANS THAN TERRORISTS TO PROP UP PUPPET RULERS AND EXPLOIT GAS AND OIL RESOURCES.

MUSEUMS? LET 'EM BURN! GET DOWN TO BASRA AND REPAIR THAT PIPELINE!

SO WHEN TILLMAN GOT KILLED BY THE AFGHAN RESISTANCE, ONE WORD NATURALLY CAME TO MIND:

UH- IDIOT?

SAP?

HERO!

DAILY NEWS

NEWS HERO!

EDITOR

With a few minor variations, the Tillman controversy followed the same trajectory as the brouhaha over "Terror Widows." First the right-wing blogs began linking to it and airing their own complaints (anti-American, treasonous, etc.) Then the Drudge Report posted it, which led to right-wing talk radio referencing it, then the daily newspapers, and finally the usual suspects on FOX: Bill O'Reilly and Sean Hannity. Once again, hundreds of God-fearing American citizens who pass as rational human beings when nowhere near a computer keyboard fired off threats of death and dismemberment in my direction. A few samples follow.

From *kmdg2@tedrallsux.com* [actual URLs deleted to protect the guilty]:

Sleep tight. I'm coming to kill you.

From matthew@tedrallsux.com:

F**k you you anti American son of a bitch. Get the f**k out of my country now! Call me you bitch if you have the balls to withstand justified criticism for your less than respectful comments about Mr. Tilman. You suck and I hope crowds chase your liberal ass out of this country. Give me a number to call you you f**king p***y ass c**t.

PS: F**k you and leave my country BITCH

From erslo@tedrallsux.com:

You are one f**ked up piece of shit. I hope someone blows your head off, you filthy c********r. Fortunately assholes like you don't live long. F**K YOU!

From a cowardly re-mailer:

Ted has a small Penis. He plays with it all day long. Thats funny isnt it?

From mayj@tedrallsux.com:

You are a LOSER! Ted Rall makes me sick! The same military that protects your ass, he has the nerve to criticize! You need to move out of this country! Leave! If you hate this country so much, move to Yemen! Your on Pat Tillman was disgusting. Why don't you take your panzie ass and join the military?! You wouln't last, you big baby! You have never served this country in any capacity, have you? You are jerk. A simple liberal idiot! You make me puke! Ted, do us all a favor and LEAVE! Move to another country pal, and see how you like it there. To never serve this country, and have the audacity to criticize somebody who gave their life for this country is despicable! You make me puke! I can I can tell you of another 1.5 million you make sick in our armed forces!

Oh, and come on down to Ft Benning, Ft Bragg, Ft Carson, Camp Lejuene, or any other military base, and write this article! Stand out in front of the base and read it, you dickhead! We would love to kick your spindly ass! It is losers like you that need to move to another country, you idiot! You hate our Government, but, you love the money you make writing stupid comic articles that mean NOTHING! LOSER!

From mreese@tedrallsux.com:

Well, Ive always considered you a commie, now you have proved it.

Eat Shit traitor.

From News6809@tedrallsux.com:

Rall you are the king of scum, I know if there is a hell you will def be there suffering like you made Pat till-mans family suffer. I hope you are No 1 when the next terrorist attack comes Have a Great day scumbag If I ever see you I will gladly spit in your face !!!!!!!!!!!!!!!!!

I was reading, tallying and deleting this bilious deluge when a reporter called from the Associated Press for comment. The result was a May 5, 2004, story titled "Rall Receives Death Threats Over Tillman Cartoon":

Cartoonist Ted Rall says he has received numerous death threats over a cartoon he did this week that satirized the media's response to the death of Pat Tillman, the former pro-football player killed in Afghanistan.

Rall said in an interview Wednesday that he has received about 6,000 e-mails in response to the cartoon, which was distributed Monday. MSNBC.com pulled the cartoon from its Web site, saying it "did not meet MSNBC.com standards of fairness and taste."

The cartoon said that Tillman "falsely believed" that the wars in Iraq and Afghanistan were linked to the Sept. 11 attacks, and that Tillman was a "cog in a low-rent occupation army that shot more innocent civilians than terrorists to prop up puppet rulers and exploit gas and oil resources."

Rall said the responses to the cartoon started out "extremely negative," with critical responses outweighing positive ones by nearly 100 to 1. But he said the tide has since turned, and now about 80 percent of the reaction has been supportive, which he called "the natural ebb and flow of this kind of thing."

Some 300 of the messages threatened Rall with "death or bodily harm," he said, and he also said he had received several death threats by phone.

Universal Press Syndicate, which distributes Rall's cartoons to about 70 newspapers, has received several e-mails from readers who objected to the content of the comic, spokeswoman Kathie Kerr said.

But Kerr also added that the syndicate often receives feedback about the political columnists and cartoonists it carries, which also include Ann Coulter, a conservative commentator, as well as the comic strips *Doonesbury* and *The Boondocks*.

Bill O'Reilly had Rall on his program on the FOX News Channel on Tuesday, and the two traded barbs over the cartoon. O'Reilly closed the show by saying that Rall "should be ashamed of what you did to Tillman."

Rall addressed the controversy on his Web site, saying his cartoon was a "reaction to the extraordinary lionizing of Mr. Tillman as a national hero."

He also criticized the media's "decision to genuflect to a cult of death," which he said was "terrifyingly similar to the cult of Palestinian suicide bombers in the Middle East and the glorious coverage given by the Japanese during World War II to fallen kamikaze fighters."

This wire service piece, syndicated to hundreds of newspapers nationwide, helped recast the debate: Cartoonist draws annoying cartoon, gets threatened with death. Is this what America has come to? Whatever happened to freedom of speech? I appeared on *Hannity & Colmes* to discuss the piece. Alan Colmes, a former stand-up comedian who plays the Washington Generals to Sean Hannity's Globetrotters as FOX's resident ersatz liberal, opened the discussion: "I think this kind of stuff gives liberals a bad name. You call [Tillman] basically an idiot and a sap for going to fight a war that you don't believe in. I'm not for the war in Iraq either, but to call someone these kinds of— or to imply these things for doing what they think is right for their country, I think is—I think it's shameful."

"You're entitled to your opinion," I replied. "I think that what happened to Mr. Tillman is tragic, not heroic. And I think it's really unfortunate to think that the right-wing media is trying to prop this guy up as an example of the kind of thing that young Americans should be."

It went downhill from there.

Colmes continued: "So you think the president—well, I don't agree with him politically, and I do think we were misled, but you think he's overtly a murderer?"

"He's not gutsy enough to do his own killing," I replied, lifting a line from *The Taking of Pelham One Two Three*. Then Hannity entered the fray.

"Ted, you're a left-wing radical nut. That's fine. You have every right to be a moron. You have every right to be thoughtless."

"Ditto."

"Here's the deal. You do this, and you call this man, who gave up millions of dollars in a contract because he was so affected by 9/11. And you do it without any thought for his family, which has already suffered, any thought for his community, which has already suffered. And you do it to make a big fat name for yourself as the great controversial cartoonist. You know what you are? You're just mean. You're a mean, selfish human being. Isn't that what it comes down to?"

"I don't claim to be a perfect guy, Sean."

"Well, you're not."

"But you've been sitting here pimping a war for the last two and a half years that has killed thousands of innocent people."

Hannity's eyes grew wide with fearful surprise at the word "pimping." I wonder why.

Postscript: In September 2004, months after the Tillman cartoon was published and digested through the zeitgeist, the publisher of *Men's Health* decided to drop my freelance comic strip about men and relationships, *The Testosterone Diaries*, as a result. *Men's Health* had never run my political cartoons and *TD* did not include political topics.

Several *Men's Health* editors unsuccessfully argued that caving into pressure from partisan political groups set a dangerous precedent. Moreover, many of the letters to the editor that prompted the publisher's decision to fire me were generated via right-wing blog sites that urged their readers to claim that they were irate subscribers, whether or not that was actually the case. I briefly considered filing a lawsuit against these sites.

New York and other states prohibit "tortious interference with contract," or injuring a business relationship using illegal means. A letter writer asking a magazine to fire a cartoonist is protected by the First Amendment. But a letter writer who threatens to cancel his subscription unless the cartoonist is fired is committing fraud unless he's really a subscriber. This type of misrepresentation, though unethical and clearly illegal, ought to be challenged in the courts.

Although a few media outlets took notice of the one-year anniversary of his death, Tillman was largely forgotten by many of the politicians and pundits to whom his story had been so useful. My follow-up cartoons, which received little commentary from an increasingly sheepish right-wing blogosphere, noted the futility of sacrificing one's life for a callous and dishonest band of political gangsters.

The right-wing media was silent.

On May 4, 2005, the *Washington Post* printed a lengthy front-page reconstruction of the circumstances of Tillman's death and the military cover-up, which included Brigadier General Gary M. Jones's conclusion that General John Abizaid knew that Tillman had been the victim of friendly fire days before recommending that he be awarded the Silver Star for events that did not occur. Jones revealed that members of Tillman's unit burned his uniform and body armor in an attempt to disguise the true cause of his death. "The fact that he was the ultimate team player and he watched his own men kill him is absolutely heartbreaking and tragic," said his mother, Mary. "The fact that they lied about it afterward is disgusting."

His father, Patrick Jr., was even angrier: "After it happened, all the people in positions of authority went out of their way to script this. They purposely interfered with the investigation, they covered it up. I think they thought they could control it, and they realized that their recruiting efforts were going to go to hell in a handbasket if the truth about his death got out. They blew up their poster boy."

At this writing the Defense Department inspector general is conducting an ongoing investigation into Tillman's death.

Reagan in Hell

Ronald Reagan died on June 5, 2004. I wrote the following on my blog: "How sad that Ronald Reagan didn't die in prison, where he belonged for starting an illegal, laughably unjustifiable war against Grenada under false pretenses (the "besieged" medical students later said they were nothing of the sort) and funneling arms to hostages during Iran-Contra. Oh, and 9/11? That was his. Osama bin Laden and his fellow Afghan 'freedom fighters' got their funding, and nasty weapons, from Reagan. A real piece of work, Reagan ruined the federal budget, trashed education, alienated our friends and allies and made us a laughingstock around the world. Hmmmm . . . sounds familiar. Anyway, I'm sure he's turning crispy brown right about now."

Talk about violating Mike Peters's diktat!

I coupled my blog entry with a column detailing Reagan's destructive legacy and a single panel depicting Reagan in hell—well, sort of.

My one-two punch was my attempt to counter a stream of elegies that were another part of the right's death cult. First there were the dead heroes of the working class: the cops and the firefighters and the passengers who fought back. Then there was the football hero who gave up everything for the Cause. And now the president who laid the groundwork for it all: the conservative tax policies, the aggressive militarism, the covert wars, and the arming of the Afghan *mujahedeen* who would someday morph into the Taliban. It was the "crispy brown" comment that really got things stirred up.

Once again, the same old pattern: Drudge, blogs, radio, dailies, AP, FOX News. And the hate mail. Always the hate mail. Why are right-wingers so obsessed with homosexuality?

A lovely missive from laprentke@tedrallsux.com:

You miserable shred of human debris.

I will pray every Sunday that you find aids in one of your lovers' asses, turn "brown & crispy", then die without taxpayer concern!

From douglasice@tedrallsux.com:

You are a c********r, Go back to the USSR, that failed like you. When you are a fag, you need to pull your head out of your ass. Do every one some good and move down to Cuba.

Thank you. Jerkweed Burn In Hell!!!!

From warology@tedrallsux.com:

You deserve a big punch in the nose. And if I ever run in to you on the street, that is exactly what you will get.

From info@tedrallsux.com:

F**k you! you c********r! . . . You piss ant twerp . . . I would shove those gay glasses up your ass . . . You C********r F**K YOU

From lwillens@tedrallsux.com:

Mother F**king low life communist faggot pig. You are as much of a virus as the aids virus. The problem with this country is you and the faggotry you practice.

From TuAl@tedrallsux.com:

You are so ugly and mean spirited I hope someone puts a bullet in the back of your head.

I returned to FOX—by now their security system had me registered as a frequent flyer—for yet another berating at the thin-lipped mouth of Sean Hannity. "You are mean!" he shouted. "You are cruel! You are thoughtless, and you are a hateful human being! You don't have a soul! And you don't care about anybody but yourself! And you do this for shock value so that your name could be noticed. You're a slob. You're an absolutely—you're a hateful human being to do this to families that are suffering. There's no excuse for it. There's no rationale for what you're doing. You're mean, cruel, and thoughtless."

"Well, there you go again, Sean." Sadly, Hannity didn't recognize the Reagan reference. The next day syndicated radio host Rush Limbaugh turned the "EIB Golden Microphone" against yours truly:

RUSH: We go to Raleigh, North Carolina. Hello, Wendy, nice to have you with us.

CALLER: Hi, Rush. I don't know that I can even get through this. I loved Reagan so much, and for four days I have just really been heartbroken, but then when I heard what Ted Rall wrote about Reagan and hoping that he was turning a crispy brown right now because of his policies in office. These things need to be told, Rush, and I'm so glad you're going to tell them because these people are the ones that are supporting the Democrats, they're supporting the liberals and this is the hate that they have, and it has nothing to do with reality, it has nothing to do with who the president was at that time. He was a great man.

RUSH: You did great, Wendy.

CALLER: I'm sorry.

RUSH: No, no, no, no, this is good. Ted Rall did write some things, I'm sure many of you have heard about it. He did say that he was sure or he hoped that Reagan was turning a crispy brown, meaning he's burning in hell for what he did to people. You know, Wendy, the best thing I can say to you at this time of your grief and your pain is probably to tell you how Reagan would react to this.

CALLER: He would have ignored it.

RUSH: He would have ignored it and he would have laughed about it, and he would have taken it as a measure of his success.

CALLER: But he can't defend himself so, Rush, you have to.

RUSH: Well, but you know, we were just discussing this in the break. Ronald Reagan was bigger than the media in life, he's bigger than the media in death, and he's certainly, Wendy, bigger than this little leprechaun, Ted Rall. This is simply Ted Rall trying to get some light shining on himself. This is one of the reasons why I have a conundrum here about talking about these people. All he's trying to do is get noticed, all he's trying to do is bask in some of the light that naturally shines on Ronald Reagan.

CALLER: But he also said those horrible things about Pat Tillman. People just really need to see the hate speech that comes out of that side.

RUSH: I think more and more people are. The media, you know, there's no condemnation of this guy.

CALLER: There isn't.

RUSH: You know, I say one little joke, one little thing they take out of context about the Abu prison photos, and it's news for two weeks, right? [Note: Limbaugh compared the torture at Abu Ghraib to college fraternity pranks.]

CALLER: Yes.

RUSH: This guy, there's no condemnation of him. In fact, there are people trying to understand what he's doing. You must understand from where he's coming, and you must understand that, well, this is a free speech era, and he's in the media, and he can say whatever he wants, and it would be terrible to shut him down, don't you think? Those are the reactions, because the thing is there are people who are glad he's saying it. There are people on his side of the aisle happy he's saying it, so that they don't have to. And the more outrageous it is, the more coverage it gets, the more successful they think it's going to be. It's just the opposite, Wendy. These people are nailing themselves in their own coffins is what's happening here. This is not how you build a movement. You do not build a movement on hate. You don't build loyalty and trust and expand your base of influence with this kind of emotion and rhetoric, epitomized by Ted Rall. And so when I first saw it, I've gotten so accustomed to these people saying things, I think they're in a contest now to see who can out outrage the other on the left. I look at this stuff, and I must tell you that a smile comes to my face when I see it, there's some anger in there, but ultimately I end up smiling because you have to know, you've lived your life, you probably haven't known anybody personally like this, have you?

At least they like me in England. In a June 14, 2004, column for the *Guardian* John Sutherland wrote: "The last time America was embroiled in a divisive war, protest mobilised in the campuses and in papers such as the *New York Times* and the *Washington Post*. Today the universities are dormant and the press too fearful about circulation to raise its voice above a dissenting murmur. Politicians keep their heads down and salute the flag—it's election year. Only the tasteless comedians (Al Franken, Michael Moore, Bill Maher, Rall) and the 'left-wing Hollywood kooks' (Barbra Streisand, Tim Robbins, Martin Sheen) are prepared to take on what they perceive as the Great Rightwing Hegemony."

Then again, perhaps a more comical, less literal, approach would have better conveyed my point about the excessive praise being heaped upon a president who'd been mediocre at best. The satirical weekly newspaper the *Onion* perfectly encapsulated the absurd phenomenon of Reagan worship with a piece titled "Reagan Pyramid Nearly Complete." A photo caption read: "Builders expect the Reagan Pyramid to be ready in time for the Great Communicator's mummification and ascension into the Afterworld upon death. Among the items to be entombed with Reagan are 2,500 MX missiles, a golden chalice of jelly beans, and his beloved servant, George Bush."

Appropriate Punishments

A rumination on what poetic justice might look like for various members of the Bush Administration were they to be removed from office and sentenced for their crimes, my July 5, 2004, cartoon, "Appropriate Punishments for Deposed Bushists," drew more fire in the weeks and months after it first appeared than when it did originally. The cartoon's critics were particularly incensed by the panel concerning Condoleezza Rice, who served as national security adviser before being promoted to secretary of state. Two years earlier, in late 2002, I had already attacked Rice (and Colin Powell's) roles as African-Americans serving the cause of racism:

That cartoon, perhaps because it appeared shortly after the Christmas holiday, attracted little notice. "Appropriate Punishments," however, was different.

On July 8 Republican syndicated columnist and blogger Michelle Malkin issued a call to arms titled "The Buck-Naked Bigotry of Ted Rall":

Ted "Bottom-feeder" Rall is at it again. His latest crude-toon includes a frame depicting Condoleezza Rice proclaiming herself Bush's "HOUSE NIGGA." A black man demands that Rice "HAND OVER HER HAIR STRAIGHTENER." His T-shirt reads "YOU'RE NOT WHITE, STUPID." The caption below the frame reads "SENT TO INNER-CITY RACIAL RE-EDUCATION CAMP." I am not going to call for a boycott of Rall's work. No. I want Universal Press Syndicate and the *Washington Post*, and all his other "mainstream" media outlets to keep publishing his pathetic scrawls and scribbles. Ted Rall, you see, is a very useful idiot. Whereas most on the left attempt to conceal their liberal racism in the drapery of "diversity" and "multiculturalism," Ted Rall is an ideological streaker. His impulsive naked bigotry is so butt-ugly, you can't help but gawk. It is raw and it is real and it is, quite helpfully, all hanging out there for the world to see.

Two weeks (!) later, Project 21, which calls itself "The National Leadership Network of Conservative African-Americans," issued a press release titled "Black Group Condemns Cartoonist for Racist Strip About Condoleezza Rice."

Actually this "black group" is nothing more than a front for a right-wing lobbying group run by an all-white board of directors, the National Center for Public Policy Research. The NCPPR, formed during the '80s to support Ronald Reagan's interventionist policies in Central America, included disgraced Washington lobbyist Jack Abramoff on its board. Its only paid employee is David Almasi, a white man who runs the "day-to-day operations" of Project 21. In an interview C-SPAN's Robb Harleston—himself black—asked Almasi: "Project 21 is a program for conservative African-Americans? You're not African-American."

The press release began:

> Because of the racially insensitive content of a recent cartoon, members of the African-American leadership network Project 21 are asking Universal Press Syndicate to cease the distribution of comics drawn by Ted Rall. Project 21 also is challenging several other civil rights–oriented groups to join in the demand.
>
> A July 1 comic by Rall suggests "appropriate punishments for deposed Bushists" that parodies alleged treatment of Iraqi detainees at the Abu Ghraib prison. The panel featuring Bush Administration national security adviser Condoleezza Rice has her saying "I was Bush's beard! His house nigga. His . . . " She is interrupted by a character wearing a shirt reading "You're not white, stupid" who says, "Now hand over your hair straightener."
>
> "Is it OK for Ted Rall to use such vile language because he's using it against a black conservative?" asks Project 21 member Michael King. "I'm beside myself with anger over this comic."
>
> Project 21 is asking Universal Press Syndicate, the distributor of Rall's comics, to immediately terminate their relationship with him. Project 21 is also asking the NAACP, the National Association of Black Journalists (NABJ), and the Rainbow/PUSH Coalition to make similar demands based on their past involvement in pressuring ESPN to fire radio talk show host Rush Limbaugh in 2003.

Ironically, I had opposed fellow liberals' attempt to stifle Limbaugh and radio talk host Dr. Laura Schlessinger, arguing that the appropriate response to speech with which one disagrees is additional speech, not censorship.

In any case, neither the NAACP nor other legitimate civil rights groups took the bait. I have no way of knowing this for certain, but I would guess that they are well aware of Project 21's status as a shell as well as my long record of opposition to racism. My syndicate issued this response:

> When we distribute opinionists—writers or cartoonists—to op-ed pages, it is with the knowledge that editors of those pages edit by selection. Most newspapers print only a few releases of any one cartoonist's or writer's work because of space constraints, subject matter, viewpoint expressed, or other editorial considera-

tions. We know that every client will not like every cartoon or column we distribute, but we do not prejudge the editorial diversity for subscribers that range from strongly conservative to strongly liberal. We assume the editors who buy the features we distribute know what works in their market and what [doesn't].

The criticism of Ted Rall's depiction of Ms. Rice obscures the fact that it is part of a larger, hyperbolic context. In the cartoon, Rall is clearly imagining unlikely scenarios that might befall a number of key people in President Bush's administration. That he exaggerates both the language and the events is a time-honored tool of satirists. Anyone who takes it literally is missing the point.

And a poster to Project 21's blog wrote: "Ted Rall is hilarious, passionate, and courageous. Any open-minded individual can see the point he's making. Blacks in the Bush cartel are tokens—to be utilized in the service of pretending to care about black issues, when nothing could be further from the truth. No? Well, try voting in Florida come next election as a black Democrat then. What's even funnier, by the way, is witnessing this sudden concern among conservatives about so called 'racism.' Quick! Someone call the NAACP!!"

Right-wingers have been working themselves into a rabid foam over "Appropriate Punishments for Deposed Bushists" ever since, using it as Exhibit A (or at least E) in their pantheon of something they call "liberal racism," which apparently means accusing conservative minorities of selling out. "If a white right-winger ever said such things about a black woman, do you think he would still be syndicated? And celebrated?"

Being a black conservative makes as much sense as being a Jewish Nazi. The right-wing base of the GOP is so aggressively racist that Republican presidential candidates have to use racist codes like speaking at Bob Jones University (or, in Ronald Reagan's case, launching his 1980 campaign in the Mississippi town where four "freedom riders" were murdered by the Klan in 1964) in order to get the GOP nomination. Context matters. African-Americans didn't complain about my cartoon because they know where I'm coming from. Besides, it didn't offend them as much as Condi Rice's close association with a racist administration.

Mainstreamed Election Results

"Appropriate Punishments" remains one of my favorite cartoons. It makes some good points and it's funny. Most important, it doesn't contain any misfires or collateral damage. It conforms to the editorial cartoonist's dictum to comfort the afflicted and afflict the comfortable. My November 4, 2004, cartoon comparing the American electorate to a public school classroom attempting to cope with "mainstreamed" children, on the other hand, was a fiasco. Not only was the attempted analogy forced to the point that few readers understood it, it reads like an attack on disabled children—in other words, an affliction of the already afflicted.

The 2004 presidential election presented American voters with a clear and simple choice. On the one hand you had John Kerry, a flip-flopping opportunist who voted for the war in Iraq and against funding it, who opposed the Vietnam War only to use his medals to run as a distinguished veteran. Then there was Bush: illegitimate, constantly lying, who had murdered more than one hundred thousand innocent people while bankrupting the treasury. I voted for Kerry. "How can 59,054,087 people be so DUMB?" asked the UK *Daily Mirror*. Disgusted by the results, I sat down the next day to convey my outrage. Looking back at it now, I probably wasn't in the best frame of mind to work my high-wire act on a piece of Bristol board.

In any event, this is what I came up with. Loosely based on my own experience in high school, I imagined the country as a classroom where the mentally disabled (playing the role of Republican voters and/or red states) were teaching the class (the rest of us).

Parents of special needs children, many of whom subscribe to newsgroups and discussion forums, circulated my cartoon as example of insensitivity and cruelty as expressed by mainstream culture against their kids. "My mainstreamed autistic son is not a malformed ball of slobber," read a typical response. Ouch.

Unlike the right-wing blogs, however, the special needs community is anything but uniformly conservative. "I thought the cartoon was pretty much on the mark," wrote one parent to the discussion group where the previous quote originated. "It's like anything else here anymore, you make fun of the establishment, or voice an opposing view, and suddenly it's disrespectful or insulting," wrote another. Nevertheless, many wrote to the *Washington Post* Web site. Others wrote to me. This polite and heartbreaking letter was typical:

> I'm sure you have received numerous e-mails about your "mentally handicapped" cartoon that appeared in the November 8 edition of the the *Washington Post*. I must admit I was taken aback by the cartoon and the offensive portrayal of a special needs student in an inclusive classroom.
>
> I looked at some of your other work and found I was generally in agreement with your philosophy so, rather than express outrage at this cartoon, I wanted to understand the message which, I admit, missed its mark with me. Perhaps you could explain the cartoon to me. While I may still not agree the depiction of the student was appropriate, I would like to understand the motivation.
>
> Individuals with special needs have such a difficult time fitting into the general population; I hope you understand why this particular cartoon would raise the hackles of those who work so hard to accomplish inclusion and acceptance for their students and family members.

As if I didn't already feel like a heel, other parent-activists sent me so many links to stories and studies about the state of mainstreaming and the dearth of adequate services for special needs kids that I felt stupid as well. Not only had my analogy been awkward and idiotic, it was based on a faulty, decades-old view of a public school system that had changed long ago. After thinking it over I decided I was wrong. I issued a public apology and admitted in interviews that my cartoon had been stupid.

What happened next didn't make me want to retract my apology, but it confirmed that our culture equates regret with weakness. On November 18, the trade journal *Editor and Publisher* reported:

> WashingtonPost.com is no longer running the cartoons of hard-hitting liberal Ted Rall. Rall said he thinks the site dropped his work because of a November 4 cartoon he did showing a drooling, mentally handicapped student taking over a classroom. "The idea was to draw an analogy to the electorate—in essence, the idiots are now running the country," he told *E&P*.
>
> "That cartoon certainly drew a significant amount of negative comment from our users," said WashingtonPost.com executive editor Doug Feaver when contacted by *E&P*. But he added that the decision to drop Rall was a "cumulative" one that had been building for a while.
>
> "Ted Rall does very interesting work," Feaver said. "Some of it is not funny to an awful lot of people. We decided at the end of the day that it just did not fit the tone we wanted at WashingtonPost.com."

I received e-mails from several parents who regretted the Post's decision. One wrote to the paper:

I've just heard that you have dropped Ted Rall's cartoons. I am the parent of an autistic child, and I, like others, was annoyed by Rall's cartoon depiction of a disabled child. But Rall was trying to make a point; he just picked an unfortunate, somewhat thoughtless way to do it. But one mistake should not lead to censorship. I hope you will reconsider your action and once again run Rall's incisive cartoons.

Another wrote:

I cannot believe that the esteemed *Washington Post*, home of the famed Watergate reporting, is caving in and canceling Ted Rall's comic. Offensive or not, one of the major reasons education is so lacking in our public schools is the policy of inclusion. Although that wasn't the primary target of Rall's cartoon, his point is well illustrated. My mother has FIVE mentally disabled children in her second grade class this year. Not only is it more than she can handle, it's a distraction to the other children in class and a serious detriment to their education. Teachers are not babysitters. Parents of mentally disabled and disturbed children often have very unrealistic views of what their children can accomplish (they're in denial) and what other people can tolerate in their children's behavior.

Rall once again had the guts to show people the ugly truth—why do you think they're so offended? Do you honestly believe retarded children don't drool, shout nonsense, and make a scene? Do you think the thousands of autistic, emotionally disturbed, and mentally disabled children aren't a cause of both fear and amusement to the other young children in a second-grade classroom?

This was another cowardly act of the media bending to the will of the bully—be that politically correct bully or that of the Christian Coalition. You're a newspaper, not a greeting card company. You're supposed to report the harsh truth, foster debate and open minds, not shirk from things people find "in poor taste." I'm sure the people who were offended by the doodles of Ted Rall were not motivated by his anti-war stance.

Mike Ervin, a columnist for the National Spinal Cord Injury Association Web site, wrote:

Just after the election, WashingtonPost.com ran a cartoon by Ted Rall. In his zeal to illustrate how, "the idiots are now running the country," as Rall would later explain . . . Disability activists wrote letters of protest to the Web site's editor, as well they should have. Soon Rall's syndicated strip was dropped. Rall's apology showed he really understood the problem. He admitted it was a "boneheaded" cartoon. "I forgot the editorial cartoonist's obligation to comfort the afflicted while afflicting the comfortable. . . . Special-needs children face a lot of challenges; they don't need, or deserve, mocking from me," he said.

Rall is usually a strong and funny voice on the political left, which has drawn him angry letters before. I fear this incident was the excuse needed by the editor to drop him.

It's great that our community can organize a response and be effective. But Rall was right when said, "Strong editorial cartoonists take risks. Sometimes they cross the line. Actions like the *Post*'s encourage the kind of timidity that has blandified not just editorial cartoons, but newspaper content overall."

I hope we haven't accidentally contributed to that.

My most controversial cartoons of the first Bush Administration, along with the body of work represented by the rest of this book, prompted conservative writers to smear me as a doctrinaire, knee-jerk leftist. Perhaps as a throwback to Richard Nixon's "White House Enemies List," the right composed lists of actors, politicians, and, yes, cartoonists they would like to have seen tossed into a gulag.

The blog Right Wing News named me number one on their 2003 list of "America's Most Annoying Liberals," writing, "It is a truly Herculean task to defeat Michael Moore in a 'most annoying' contest, but Ted Rall, a Marxist who does cartoons for the *New York Times* and writes columns for Yahoo!, is certainly up for it. Just consider that Rall certainly doesn't support our troops." Marxist? Where'd they get that? (I'd only made number eight in 2002: "The words 'bad-natured punk' describe Ted Rall as well as any.")

New York Press, the entropic right-wing free weekly, named me second on its own list of "Most Loathsome New Yorkers." They took a different tack, pretending to dislike me because I was bad for the left: "Much like Loathsome New Yorker Number Three, Michael Moore, Ted Rall's attempts at political commentary and liberal activism do more harm to the cause than any amount of conservative clampdown." How nice of them to care. Finally right-wing pundit Bernard Goldberg wrote a best-selling book that was nothing more than a list of *100 People Who Are Screwing Up America*. I made number fifteen, just ahead of Senator John Edwards and the Reverend Al Sharpton, based primarily on Goldberg's descriptions of my "dirty half-dozen" cartoons. Moore was number one.

Longtime readers know that I was just as fierce a critic of the Clinton Administration. I go after Democrats with the same glee as Republicans. That, after all, is my job. But Democrats have been out of power long enough that nobody remembers that. Being an equal-opportunity critic isn't the best way to make friends.

I'll let Working for Change's Bill Berkowitz have the last word: "Do Rall's cartoons and commentary occasionally stray from civil political discourse? You bet. Can he be insensitive and mean-spirited? On occasion. However, in an age where prisoners are mistreated at home and tortured abroad, where civilians are killed indiscriminately in the name of a permanent war against terrorism, and where administration utterances make used car salesmen look like principled truth-tellers, the boundaries of what passes as 'civilized' political debate must be challenged. And that's what Rall does."

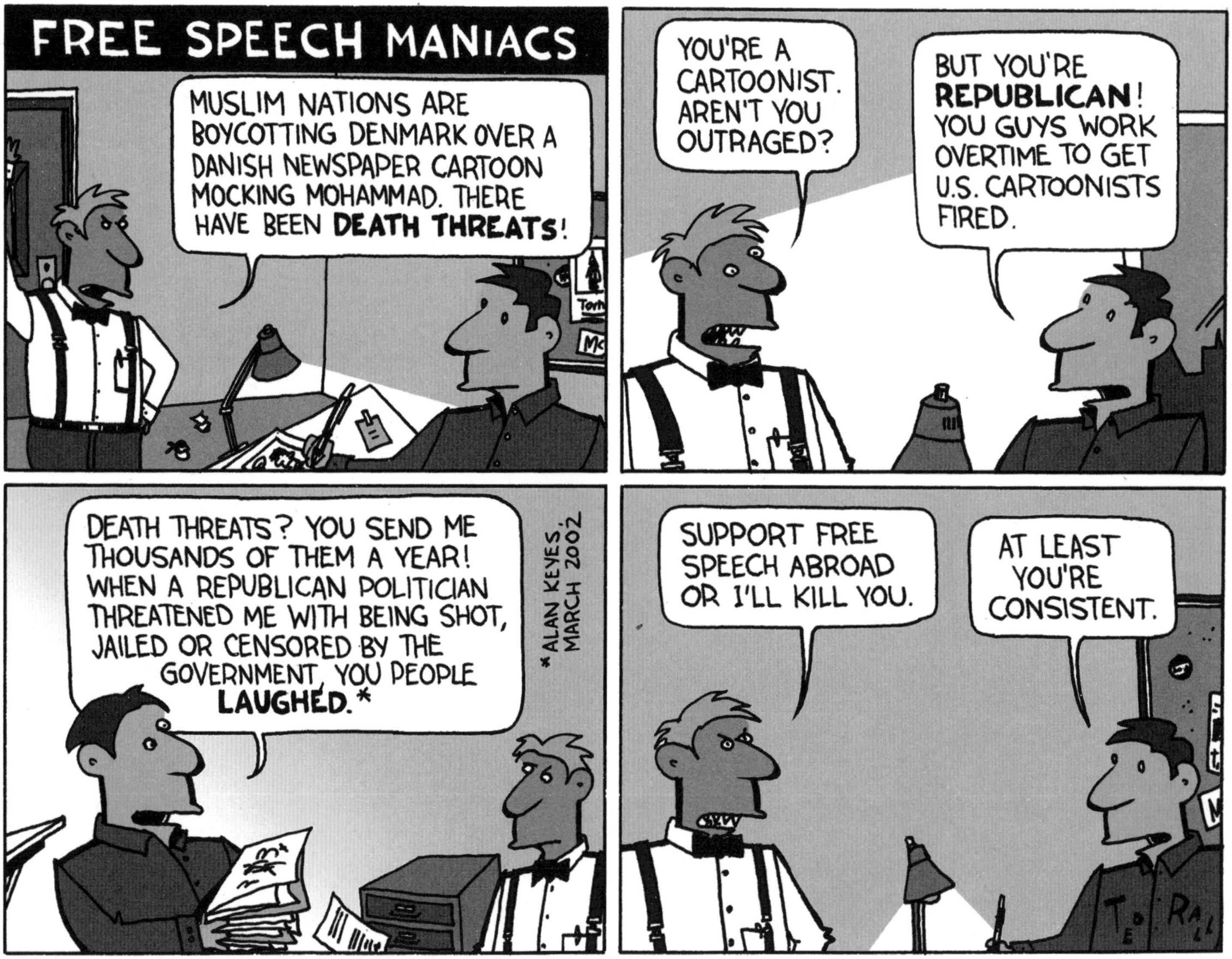
FREE SPEECH MANIACS
MUSLIM NATIONS ARE BOYCOTTING DENMARK OVER A DANISH NEWSPAPER CARTOON MOCKING MOHAMMAD. THERE HAVE BEEN **DEATH THREATS**!
YOU'RE A CARTOONIST. AREN'T YOU OUTRAGED?
BUT YOU'RE **REPUBLICAN**! YOU GUYS WORK OVERTIME TO GET U.S. CARTOONISTS FIRED.
DEATH THREATS? YOU SEND ME THOUSANDS OF THEM A YEAR! WHEN A REPUBLICAN POLITICIAN THREATENED ME WITH BEING SHOT, JAILED OR CENSORED BY THE GOVERNMENT, YOU PEOPLE **LAUGHED**.*
* ALAN KEYES, MARCH 2002
SUPPORT FREE SPEECH ABROAD OR I'LL KILL YOU.
AT LEAST YOU'RE CONSISTENT.
TED RALL

WHY THERE'S ABSOLUTELY NO FUCKING WAY WE'LL EVER JUST GET OVER IT!

DURING THE 2000 FLORIDA RECOUNT CRISIS, I ASKED MY LAWYER PALS WHAT WOULD HAPPEN.

> THE FLORIDA SUPREME COURT HAS RULED FOR A RECOUNT. DOES THAT SETTLE IT?

THEIR ANSWER WAS ALWAYS THE SAME.

> YUP. THE U.S. SUPREME COURT CAN'T HEAR THE CASE BECAUSE, AS A FEDERAL COURT, IT DOESN'T HAVE JURISDICTION OVER ELECTIONS, WHICH ARE RUN BY THE STATES.

FROM THE MOMENT THE U.S. SUPREME COURT AGREED TO HEAR *BUSH V. GORE*, THE ELECTION WAS COMPROMISED.

> SOMEONE HAD TO DO SOMETHING.

> THIS CAN'T GO ON FOREVER!

NEWS

EVEN IF THEY HADN'T SUSPENDED THE RECOUNT

EVEN IF NEWS-PAPER RECOUNTS HAD PROVEN THAT BUSH WOULD'VE WON ANYWAY

> DIDN'T THEY?

> NOT IN 7 OF 8 COUNT-ING METHODS.

EVEN IF...

> BUT A SANE ONE.

> GOT ME THERE.

EVEN IF THE LATE/ILLEGAL MILITARY BALLOTS HAD BEEN INVALIDATED

ARMED FORCES
NOV 23 2000
POST OFFICE

EVEN IF THEY'D ENSURED THAT GORE HAD "WON"

> ...THE CONST-ITUTION OF THE UNITED STATES...

...THEN GORE WOULD BE AN UN-ELECTED, TREASON-OUS COUP LEADER.

A déclassé take on the argument that people need guns to stay safe.

Many cartoonists don't understand which words get bolded and which don't.

Better to be told off than brushed off.

Afghanistan is a classic example of proxy warfare by distant nations whose populations never have to suffer.

ENOUGH IS ENOUGH! IT'S TIME TO PUT AN END TO
SPECIAL PRIVILEGES FOR BLACKS

Inspired by the Paul Kelly song "Special Treatment" about Australian aborigines,
this cartoon examines the argument that blacks have it too easy in America.

This "what if" about an Al Gore who leads a Gaullist-style resistance movement became a recurring feature over the next few years. I ended it when he decided not to run again in 2004.

Two boxes, one good and one bad.

CASH IN BIG ON THE GOVERNMENT GIVEAWAY OF THE CENTURY:
ENROLL IN SCHOOL OF BODILY FLUID ARTS

MY ART CAREER WAS NOWHERE. CHICKS CROSSED THE STREET **AND** TURNED THE CORNER TO AVOID ME. ALL THAT CHANGED AFTER I GOT MY **B.B.F.A.** — BACHELOR OF BODILY FLUID ARTS.

S.B.F.A. TURNED ME ON TO THE EXPLODING FIELDS OF FECAL-, URINE-, VOMIT- AND BLOOD-BASED ARTS. SMEARING A TURD ON A CANVAS TURNS ORDINARY ART INTO CONTROVERSIAL, TAXPAYER-FUNDED AGITPROP STATEMENTS.

NO.1   NO.2

"BEST OF ALL, I'M SAVING A **FORTUNE** ON ACRYLICS AND CHARCOALS!"

GO AWAY! I'M MAKING ART SUPPLIES!

SCART

FORTUNE

CHOOSE FROM THESE MAJORS:

TO THE UNSCHOOLED EYE, IT LOOKS LIKE PORNOGRAPHY. BUT LOOK — I USED PUKE INSTEAD OF INDIA INK!

GRAPHIC GRAPHICS

NICE PULITZER PRIZE!

THANKS! I GOT IT FOR MY "FROZEN-PEE BUDDHA (3RD IN SERIES)."

LE

URINARY SCULPTURE

IT'S BOTH PROFOUND AND RELEVANT — AT THE SAME TIME!

DEFECATION DESECRATION

COMING THIS FALL: SCRATCH 'N' SNIFF PAINTING!

TED RALL

I still seethe at having been rejected for a grant by the National Endowment for the Arts on the grounds that "cartoons are not an art form."

I like this cartoon for its atypical take on an old argument.

Bush attempted to jump-start the recession-ravaged economy by cutting $300 checks to every American. The cost was high but the benefits trivial.

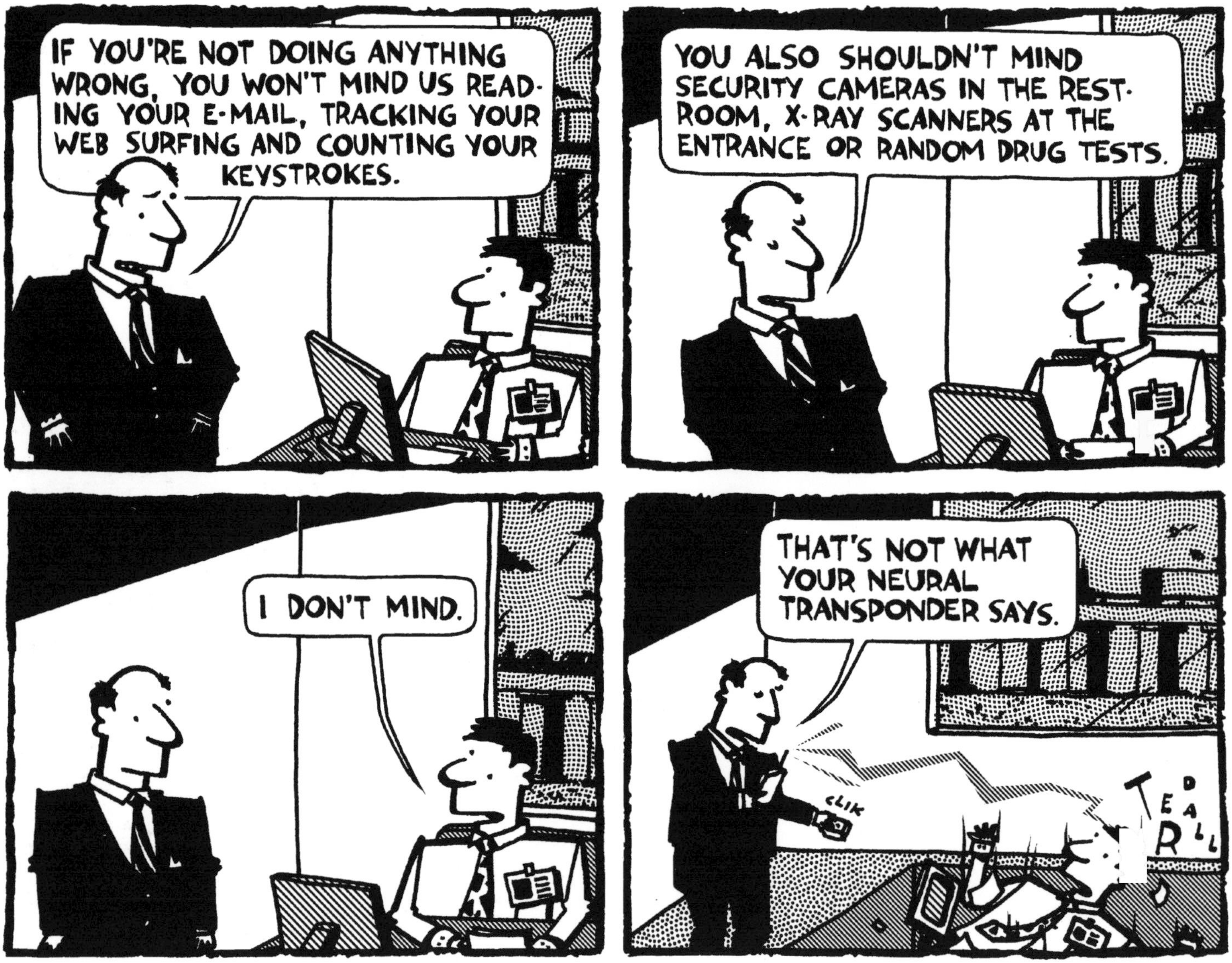
IF YOU'RE NOT DOING ANYTHING WRONG, YOU WON'T MIND US READING YOUR E-MAIL, TRACKING YOUR WEB SURFING AND COUNTING YOUR KEYSTROKES.
YOU ALSO SHOULDN'T MIND SECURITY CAMERAS IN THE RESTROOM, X-RAY SCANNERS AT THE ENTRANCE OR RANDOM DRUG TESTS.
I DON'T MIND.
THAT'S NOT WHAT YOUR NEURAL TRANSPONDER SAYS.
CLIK

There is no left in America, only a jury-rigged amalgamation of disparate special-interest groups.

This cartoon, drawn a week before 9/11 in New York City, returns to a favorite topic, paranoia.

Possibly the first joke about 9/11 published in an American newspaper, September 18, 2001's "Jihad Slacker" reacted to the news that a twentieth hijacker had missed his date with death.

Firefighters, police officers, the Port Authority of New York, and even New Jersey bureaucrats were lauded as heroes after 9/11.

This one was prompted by several cartoonists' decision, after years of decrying politics as pointless and trite, to dedicate themselves to political commentary after 9/11.

AS THE WAR MOVES ON TO WHEREVER, AMERICANS ARE
PITCHING IN FOR A BETTER TOMORROW

KEVIN JACKSON DOESN'T KNOW IT YET, BUT HE'S GIVING UP HIS COLLEGE EDUCATION TO PAY FOR THE BOMBING OF TORA BORA, AFGHANISTAN!

WITHOUT KEVIN'S SACRIFICE, WE MIGHT *NEVER* HAVE CAUGHT OSAMA BIN LADEN. THANKS, YOU HERO YOU!

RACHEL KELLER WILL DIE OF CANCER. WHY? TO HELP FUND THE AIRLINE BAILOUT!

WHAT'S THE USE OF A NATIONAL HEALTH PLAN IF YOU CAN'T FLY TO SEE YOUR DOCTOR?

UNITED WE BLAND

FELICIA PATTERSON HASN'T EVEN BEEN BORN YET, BUT SHE'LL BE RAPED BY A PREMATURELY RELEASED MENTAL PATIENT—SO THE RICH CAN GET THEIR TAX CUT!

SURE IT'S *INCONVENIENT*—BUT WE'LL NEVER DEFEAT TERRORISM UNLESS WE HAVE THE RIGHT BUDGET PRIORITIES.

ROBERT LEBON WON'T HESITATE TO TAKE A 0.3% REDUCTION IN INVESTMENT INCOME—LOOK OUT, SADDAM!

THIS IS AMERICA DAMMIT! WE'RE ALL IN THIS TOGETHER!

ANYWAY, THE TAX CUT MORE THAN COVERS IT.

TED RALL

Based on a genuine miscommunication about the Rimbaud-Rambo homonym.

The disconnect between American rhetoric and policy widened into a vast canyon after the attacks on New York and Washington.

CONFUSION, CHAOS AND ALLITERATION... HERE'S YOUR GUIDE TO
UNDERSTANDING EDITORIAL CARTOONS

Panel 1: FIRST AND FOREMOST, CARTOONS ARE ALWAYS 100% TRUE. CARTOONISTS SHUN HYPERBOLE AND DISTORTION TO BRING YOU THE VERY BEST IN JOURNALISM *VERITÉ*.

GENERALISSIMO HAT
EAR
EPAULETTE
CARTOON OF GEORGE W. BUSH
PHOTO OF GEORGE W. BUSH

Panel 2: GOOD CARTOONS ARE ALWAYS FAIR, AS WELL AS SENSITIVE. COULD SOMEONE BE OFFENDED? IF YES, IT'LL MAKE FOR A TERRIBLE CARTOON.

WHAT?! THIS CARTOON TAKES ISSUE WITH THE EFFICIENCY OF **POSTAL WORKERS**!

HOW **MEAN**! SO MUCH FOR THAT "CARTOONIST'S" CAREER!

ACTUAL DEPICTION OF PULITZER DISCUSSION

Panel 3: SINCE ALL STRONG OPINIONS ARE INHERENTLY ARBITRARY, EVERY CARTOON HAS ITS EQUAL AND OPPOSITE COUNTERPART.

I'M A DUMB NON-ELECTED IDIOT.

I AM ARTIC-ULATE AND ELECTED.

SINCE ALL STRONG OPINIONS ARE INHERENTLY ARBITRARY, EVERY CARTOON HAS ITS EQUAL AND OPPOSITE COUNTERPART.

Panel 4: BUT FORGET ALL THAT: EDITORIAL CARTOONISTS ALWAYS HAVE TO BE FUNNY!

SEE, THE BEAVER LABELED "CITY POLICE" IS BUILDING A DAM LABELED "STREET PATROLS."

AND THE WATER IS LABELED "RISING CRIME". NOW **THAT'S** FUNNY!

DAI

Cartoonists receive a lot of hate mail from people who obviously require a tutorial on the editorial cartoon format.

A piece for *Gear* magazine in response to Republican control of the executive, legislative, and judicial branches of government.

A spate of child kidnappings increased parents' paranoia.

After Generations X and Y, what?

Tech-savvy programmers began producing pornography, including fake "child" porn, without using live human subjects.

Vegetarians argue that meat is contaminated by toxins released into the bloodstreams of terrified cattle at slaughter.

What will you think about when you die?

Exposed midriffs appear to be here to stay. Could this be next?

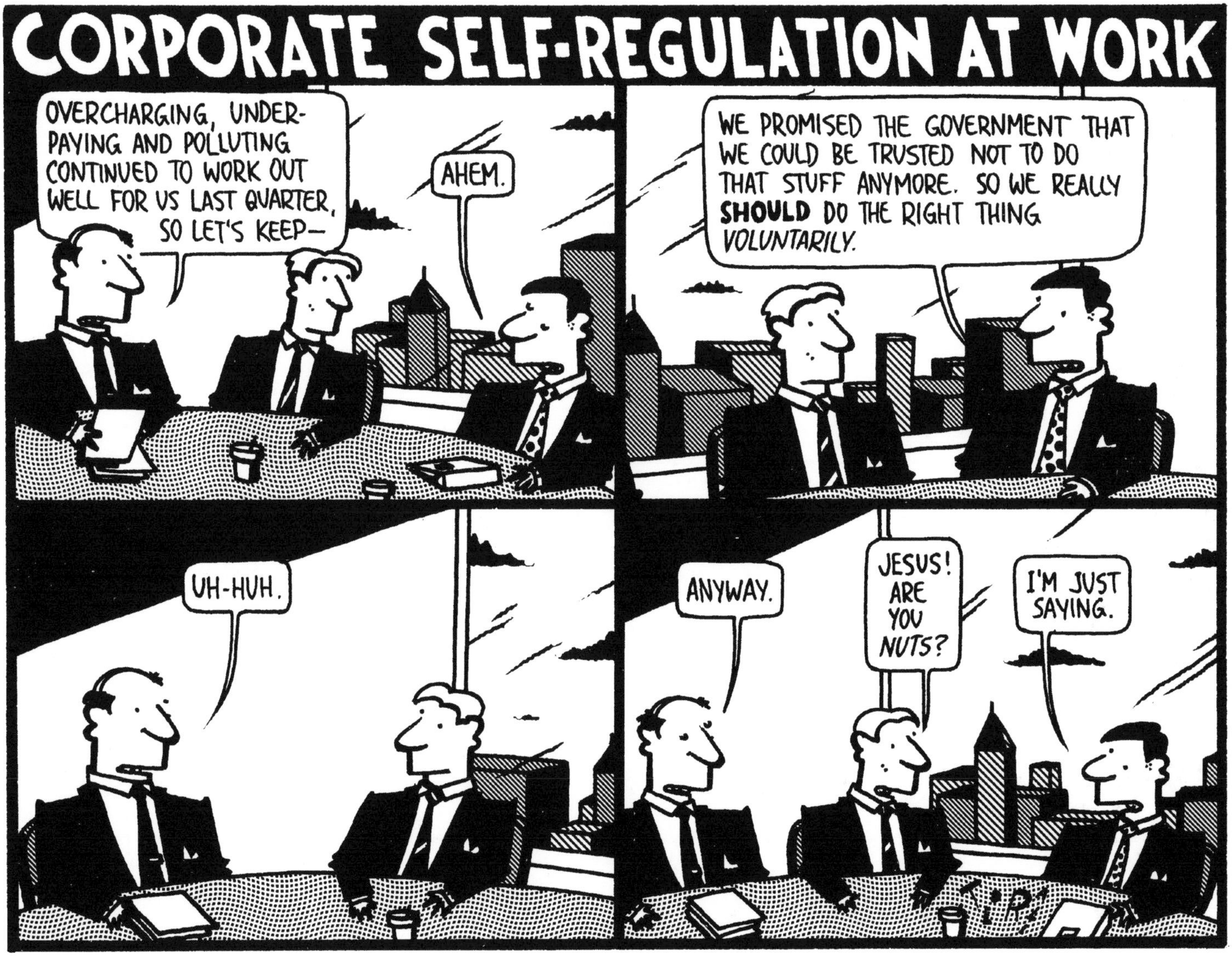
CORPORATE SELF-REGULATION AT WORK
OVERCHARGING, UNDER-PAYING AND POLLUTING CONTINUED TO WORK OUT WELL FOR US LAST QUARTER, SO LET'S KEEP—
AHEM.
WE PROMISED THE GOVERNMENT THAT WE COULD BE TRUSTED NOT TO DO THAT STUFF ANYMORE. SO WE REALLY **SHOULD** DO THE RIGHT THING *VOLUNTARILY.*
UH-HUH.
ANYWAY.
JESUS! ARE YOU *NUTS?*
I'M JUST SAYING.

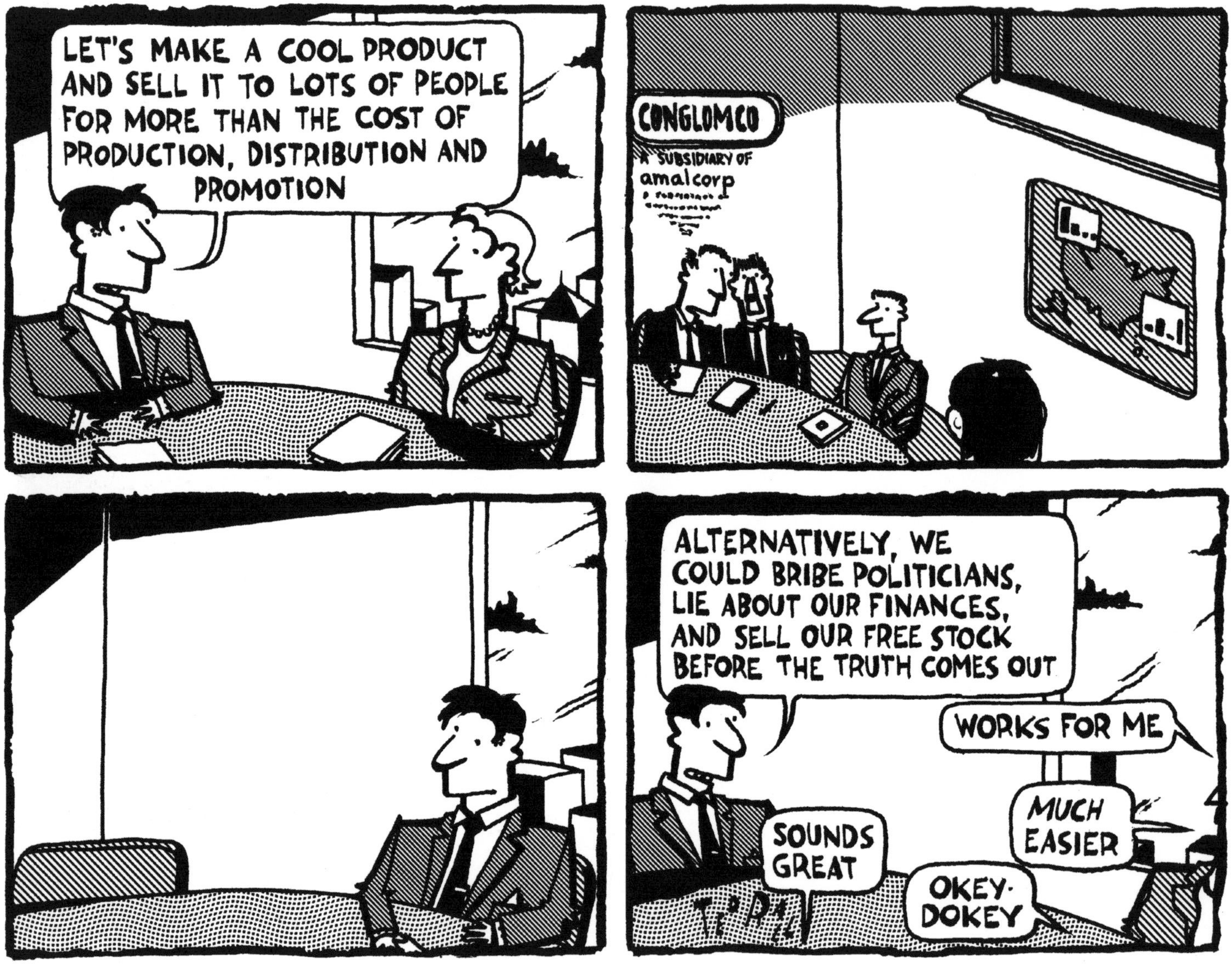
LET'S MAKE A COOL PRODUCT AND SELL IT TO LOTS OF PEOPLE FOR MORE THAN THE COST OF PRODUCTION, DISTRIBUTION AND PROMOTION
CONGLOMCO
A SUBSIDIARY OF
amalcorp
ALTERNATIVELY, WE COULD BRIBE POLITICIANS, LIE ABOUT OUR FINANCES, AND SELL OUR FREE STOCK BEFORE THE TRUTH COMES OUT
WORKS FOR ME
MUCH EASIER
SOUNDS GREAT
OKEY-DOKEY

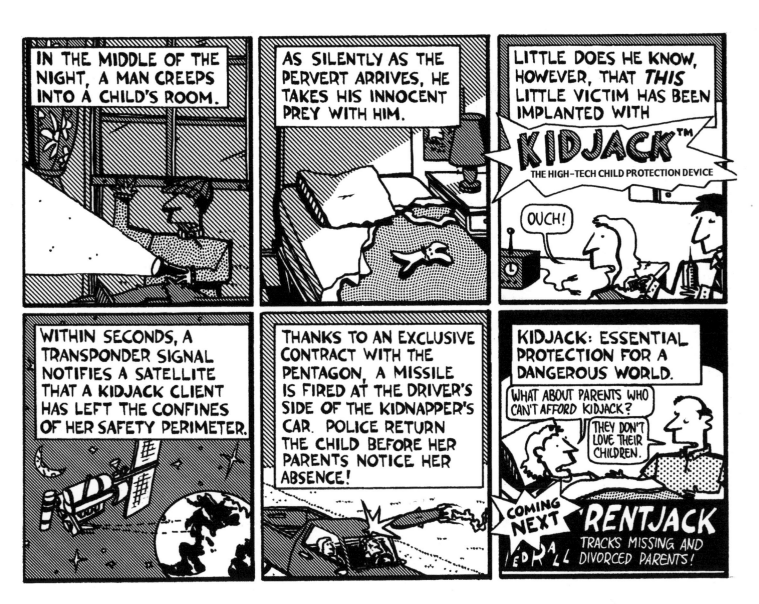

Another take on the kidnapping phenomenon, this one focusing on new technology that parents and pet owners use to track their charges via GPS technology.

August 2002: Bush threatened to invade Iraq.

NOT SO LONG AGO, A WOMAN SO WILLING TO FIGHT DEFORESTATION THAT SHE WAS WILLING TO RISK HER SOCIAL LIFE CLIMBED A TREE AND VOWED TO STAY UNTIL THE TIMBER INDUSTRY PROMISED TO STOP DOING BAD THINGS. THIS IS HER STORY.

diARY of A TREE SiTTER

DAY 1: I, DEBRAH JESSIKA PULASKI, VOW TO STAY IN MY SYCAMORE UNTIL EVIL EARTH PLUNDERERS PLEDGE NOT TO CUT IT DOWN. I AM YOURS, GREAT EARTH MOTHER!

WHY DO WE ALL LOOK LIKE BJÖRK?

DAY 3: WREN CALLED FROM THE TREE SITTERS COLLECTIVE. "DEBRAH?" SHE COUNSELED ME. "WHAT KIND OF NAME IS THAT?"

HEAR THIS, OH GODDESS— DEBRAH IS DEAD! I CONSECRATE MYSELF "DEW"!

YOUR SOY BURGERS ARE HERE.

DAY 4: IT'S COLD UP HERE! WET, TOO. AS SOON AS WE WIN THE WAR ON TREEORISM WE'VE GOT TO DO SOMETHING ABOUT THESE BUGS.

DIE!

DAY 7: STILL NO LUMBER BADDIES. OF COURSE, I AM IN A CITY PARK!

DEW. D-E-W. THE WASHINGTON POST GOT IT WRONG.

YOU KNOW, YOU LOOK JUST LIKE BJÖRK.

DAY 10: NATURE IS AMAZING! I NEVER THOUGHT I'D SEE A THUNDERSTORM THIS CLOSE!

WHOA!

YOU SHOULD HAVE SMELLED HER BEFORE THE LIGHTNING STRIKE.

Environmental activists squat on old-growth trees to prevent lumber companies from cutting them down.

Democracy became something Americans watch on television.

Thousands of troops and tons of equipment flooded into the Persian Gulf in late 2002.
The effect was that of a slow-motion surprise attack.

The Generalissimo's New Clothes

THERE was a Generalissimo who was so excessively fond of new clothes that he spent all his money on them. He cared nothing about his soldiers, nor for the theater except for the sake of showing off his new clothes.

One day two swindlers came to visit the Generalissimo. They sold him a set of clothes which nobody, including the Generalissimo, could see. But so colorful and convincing were their descriptions of those clothes that he persuaded himself that he could see them.

Then the Generalissimo took off all his clothes and went out to walk in his procession in his new invisible "clothes." Everybody in the streets exclaimed, "How beautiful the Generalissimo's clothes are!"

"But he has got nothing on," said a little child. The Generalissimo winced, for he knew that it was true.

Thus he ordered his minister of homeland security to beat the crap out of the little boy and everyone who agreed with him and to throw them all into a dark dungeon, where they were forever denied access to legal counsel.

And so the mighty Generalissimo and all the people who weren't in prison lived happily ever after.

Other cartoonists made this comparison—usually later than '02—but I like the way this version reads.

Americans discussed their "gut feelings," based on nothing, about whether or not Iraq possessed the purported weapons of mass destruction.

IN A NEW EFFORT TO STIMULATE THE ECONOMY, THE BUSH ADMINISTRATION IS ASKING AMERICANS TO LET IT LOOT PUBLIC LANDS AND BUILDINGS.

FREE TRAPPED STUFF

FREE TRAPPED STUFF

FREE TRAPPED STUFF

FREE TRAPPED STUFF

INCREDIBLE WEALTH IS LOCKED UP—WASTED—IN GOVERNMENT PROPERTY. *RELEASE* THAT *TRAPPED STUFF* AND LET IT WORK FOR **AMERICA!**

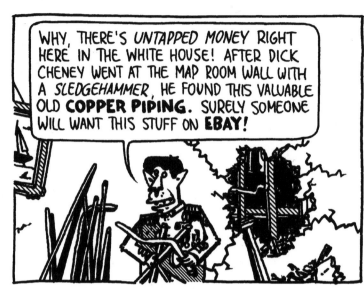

WHY, THERE'S *UNTAPPED MONEY* RIGHT HERE IN THE WHITE HOUSE! AFTER DICK CHENEY WENT AT THE MAP ROOM WALL WITH A *SLEDGEHAMMER*, HE FOUND THIS VALUABLE OLD **COPPER PIPING.** SURELY SOMEONE WILL WANT THIS STUFF ON **EBAY!**

A LOT OF THESE **OLD TREES** WILL BRING IN *BIG BUCKS* AS *LUMBER.* WE'RE STRIP-MINING THE SOUTH LAWN. AND YOU WOULDN'T **BELIEVE** WHAT WE'RE GETTING FOR **19TH-CENTURY FIXTURES!**

AS USUAL, EVERYONE AGREES THAT THEFTI-NOMICS IS A GOOD IDEA. THE ONLY AREA OF DISPUTE IS HOW TO CARRY IT OUT.

THE LIBRARY OF CONGRESS BELONGED TO *ALL OF US!* THE CASH FROM SELLING IT TO BARNES & NOBLE SHOULD BE SHARED EQUALLY!

DON'T BE SELFISH... I THOUGHT OF THIS SCHEME, AND I'M KEEPING THE *DOUGH!*

NATIONAL MONUMENT

FOR SALE

Oddly presaging the looting of Baghdad three months later, here I viewed members of the Bush Administration as "busting out" the government like *Goodfellas*-style gangsters.

FREAK-SHOW POLITICS

ANYONE WHO BURNS AN AMERICAN FLAG SHOULD BE KILLED!

OH, RIGHT. LIKE YOU SEE THAT HAPPENING SO OFTEN WE NEED A CONSTITUTIONAL AMENDMENT!

ONLY 6 PARTIAL-BIRTH ABORTIONS HAPPEN A YEAR, BUT EVERY LIFE IS SO SACRED IT'S WORTH KILLING OVER!

IF WE BAN EVEN THE MOST EXTREME FORM OF ABORTION, NORMAL ABORTION WILL BE NEXT!

PRO CHOICE

CLONING HUMAN BEINGS SHOULD BE BANNED... OTHERWISE DARWINISM IS DOOMED!

NOT ONLY IS CLONING NOT HAPPENING IN SIGNIFICANT NUMBERS, I DEMAND THE RIGHT TO DO SO!

I LOST MY JOB.

TEdRALL

Americans' real problems are ignored by a media obsessed with debates over trivia.

OUR LEGISLATIVE SYSTEM AT WORK

ONE PARTY PROPOSES A STUPID LAW.

H.R. 3018, THE INSTITUTIONAL INSIPIDITY REVENUE ACT OF 2003, WILL SAVE AMERICA $40.

H.R. 301 INSTIT

THE OTHER PARTY COUNTERS WITH A MORE EXTREME VERSION OF THE BILL.

THEY'RE KILLING US IN THE POLLS!

DON'T WORRY— WE'LL STEAL THE ISSUE FROM THEM.

THE STUPID BILL IS SIGNED INTO LAW.

IT'S GREAT TO SEE THE SPIRIT OF BIPARTISANSHIP RESULT IN SMART LEGISLATION!

AFTER THE LAW CAUSES PROBLEMS, THE OPPOSITION PARTY BLAMES ITS RIVALS FOR ITS DUMB IDEA.

THEIR BILL **COST** TAXPAYERS $85!

2003-2006 PROJECTED

THE MAJORITY PARTY COUNTERS THAT THE OPPOSITION IS TO BLAME FOR FAILING TO OFFER AN ALTERNATIVE.

THEY **KNEW** IT WASN'T GONNA WORK BUT THEY WENT ALONG ANYWAY!

ONE PARTY PROPOSES A LAW TO REPAIR PROBLEMS CAUSED BY THAT EARLIER STUPID LAW.

SO H.R. 3019 WILL REVERSE THE FOLLIES OF THE PAST AND SAVE AMERICA **$300!**

TED RALL

86

The logic of preemption allows one to justify the invasion of the least threatening place on earth, Greenland.

NOW ANYONE CAN BECOME A MASTER LITIGATOR... THANKS TO

JURY SELECTION MADE E-Z

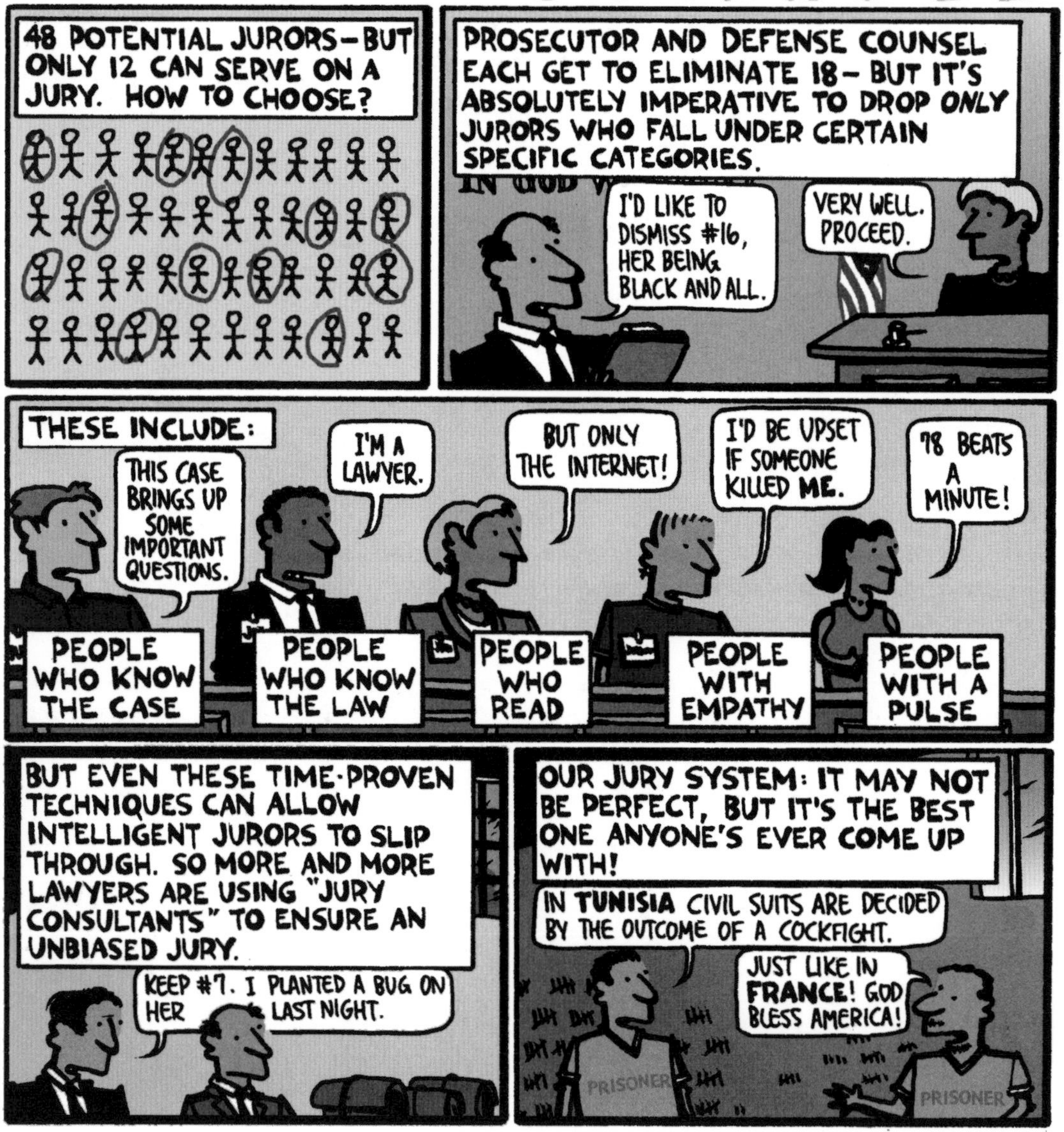
48 POTENTIAL JURORS—BUT ONLY 12 CAN SERVE ON A JURY. HOW TO CHOOSE?
PROSECUTOR AND DEFENSE COUNSEL EACH GET TO ELIMINATE 18—BUT IT'S ABSOLUTELY IMPERATIVE TO DROP ONLY JURORS WHO FALL UNDER CERTAIN SPECIFIC CATEGORIES.
I'D LIKE TO DISMISS #16, HER BEING BLACK AND ALL.
VERY WELL. PROCEED.
THESE INCLUDE:
THIS CASE BRINGS UP SOME IMPORTANT QUESTIONS.
PEOPLE WHO KNOW THE CASE
I'M A LAWYER.
PEOPLE WHO KNOW THE LAW
BUT ONLY THE INTERNET!
PEOPLE WHO READ
I'D BE UPSET IF SOMEONE KILLED ME.
PEOPLE WITH EMPATHY
78 BEATS A MINUTE!
PEOPLE WITH A PULSE
BUT EVEN THESE TIME-PROVEN TECHNIQUES CAN ALLOW INTELLIGENT JURORS TO SLIP THROUGH. SO MORE AND MORE LAWYERS ARE USING "JURY CONSULTANTS" TO ENSURE AN UNBIASED JURY.
KEEP #7. I PLANTED A BUG ON HER LAST NIGHT.
OUR JURY SYSTEM: IT MAY NOT BE PERFECT, BUT IT'S THE BEST ONE ANYONE'S EVER COME UP WITH!
IN TUNISIA CIVIL SUITS ARE DECIDED BY THE OUTCOME OF A COCKFIGHT.
JUST LIKE IN FRANCE! GOD BLESS AMERICA!
PRISONER
PRISONER

INGENUITY

JUST 8 YEARS AFTER THE FIRST FLIGHT, SOMEONE HAD AN IDEA:

WE COULD DROP EXPLOSIVES ON PEOPLE WHILE REMAINING SAFELY ALOFT!

GRAND!

DURING THE ITALIAN-TURKISH WAR IN NORTH AFRICA IN 1911, LT. GIULIO GAVOTTI DROPPED 4 GRENADES ON A CAMP AT AIN ZARA, LIBYA.

MANGI LA MORTE, CANI TURCI!

THIS "BOMBING" TECHNIQUE PROVED INITIALLY UNPOPULAR.

ONLY A **CAD** WOULD FIGHT A WAR USING SUCH BARBARISM! I SAY!!

BOMBS KILL HUNDREDS

AERIAL BOMBARDMENT BEGAN IN EARNEST IN WORLD WAR I, CULMINATING WITH A BRUTAL RAID ON GERMAN TROOPS IN EASTERN FRANCE.

SINCE WORLD WAR II, U.S. FORCES HAVE BOMBED AN ESTIMATED 4,029,000 INNOCENT PEOPLE TO DEATH.

IS THIS WHAT WE HAD IN MIND, ORVILLE?

HELL IF I KNOW.

TEDRALL

Interestingly, this cartoon provoked little controversy when published.

Promises of quick rebuilding evaporated as Iraqis under American occupation experienced shortages of water and gasoline far worse than under the deposed Saddam Hussein regime.

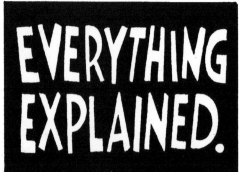

EVERYTHING EXPLAINED.

WE TRIED THIS SAME EXACT STUPID IDEA BEFORE, AND IT WORKED OUT GREAT!

THAT'S A LIE!

I **LOVE** THE PRESIDENT'S STUPID PLAN. LAST TIME IT MADE ME **RICH**!

NO, IT DIDN'T.

DON'T YOU REMEMBER? YOU LOST ALL YOUR MONEY AND YOUR DOG **DIED**! THAT'LL HAPPEN AGAIN!

CHECK OUT THE **NUT**! MR. **PARANOID** WOULD RATHER DO **NOTHING** THAN SOMETHING STUPID!

HAW!

LOON!

WHAT DO YOU THINK ABOUT THE STUPID IDEA?

GRRRR... NO COMMENT.

92% FAVOR STUPID IDEA

YEARS PASS.

EVERYONE THOUGHT THE STUPID IDEA WAS A SMART IDEA. NOW IT'S OBVIOUS THAT IT'S A DISASTER.

NOT EVERYONE! NOT ME! I KNEW!

U.S.A. IN RUINS

IT'S BAD ENOUGH THAT YOU SUPPORTED AN IDEA THAT DESTROYED EVERYTHING. DON'T MAKE THINGS WORSE BY **LYING** ABOUT IT!

The United States opened a new gulag archipelago of secret concentration camps spanning the world, from Bagram in Afghanistan to Abu Ghraib in Iraq to Guantánamo Bay, Cuba.

Disaster in Iraq and Afghanistan provoked Clinton nostalgia.

No one understood this obscure historical reference to a famed drawing of Holy Roman Emperor Henry IV, who was forced by Pope Gregory VII to wait three days in the snow at Canossa in January 1077 while awaiting pardon for denying his authority.

Who are you going to believe, yourself or the experts?

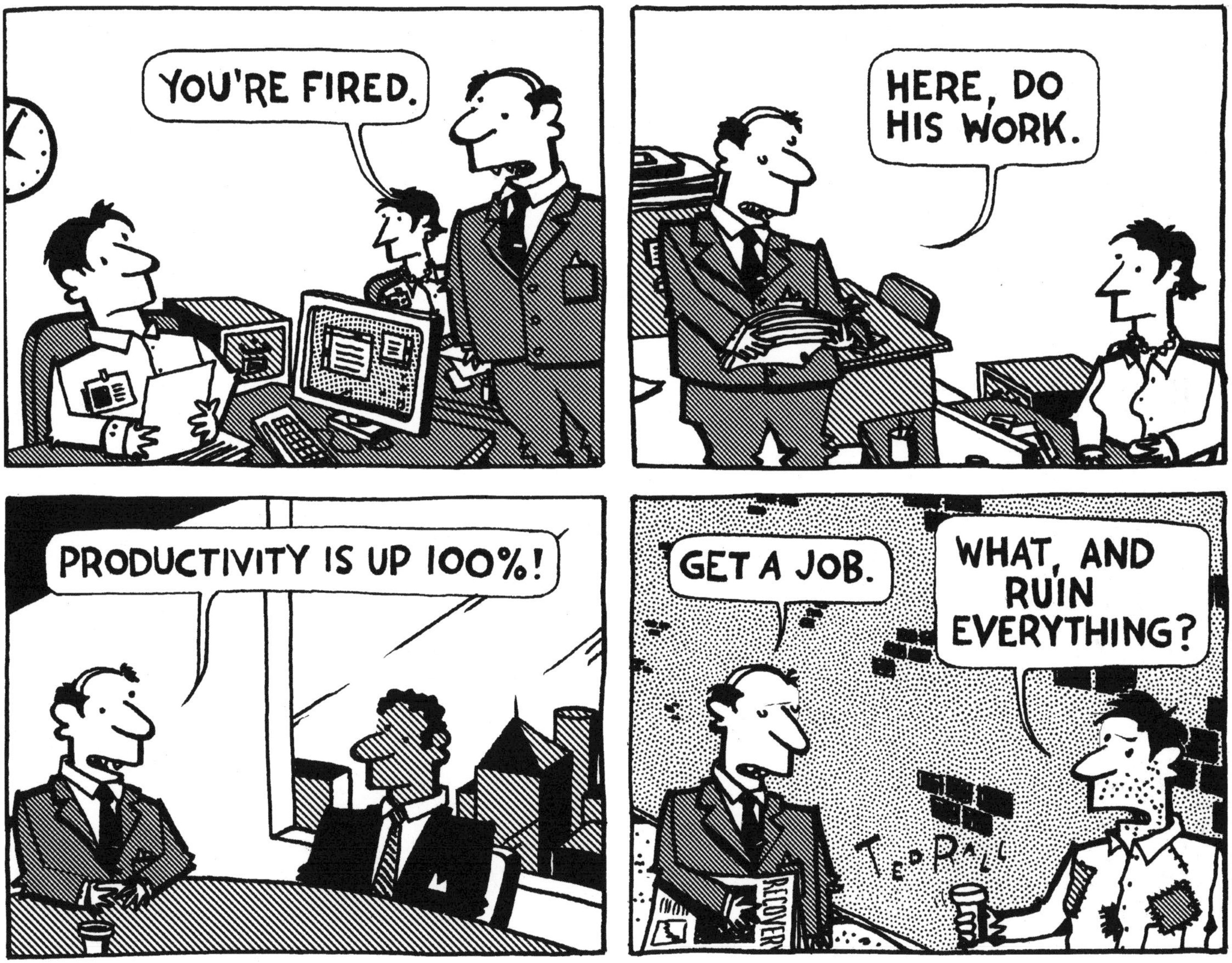
YOU'RE FIRED.
HERE, DO HIS WORK.
PRODUCTIVITY IS UP 100%!
GET A JOB.
WHAT, AND RUIN EVERYTHING?
RECOVERY
TED RALL

The United States followed failed trade pacts with Mexico and Canada with similar agreements with Central and South America.

Nearly a year after the invasion of Iraq, people began debating whether Bush's doctrine of preemptive warfare was a good idea.

California Congressman Gary Condit fell under suspicion when his intern Chandra Levy, with whom he had been having an affair, went missing. Cases of missing women, especially attractive ones, soon became a media staple.

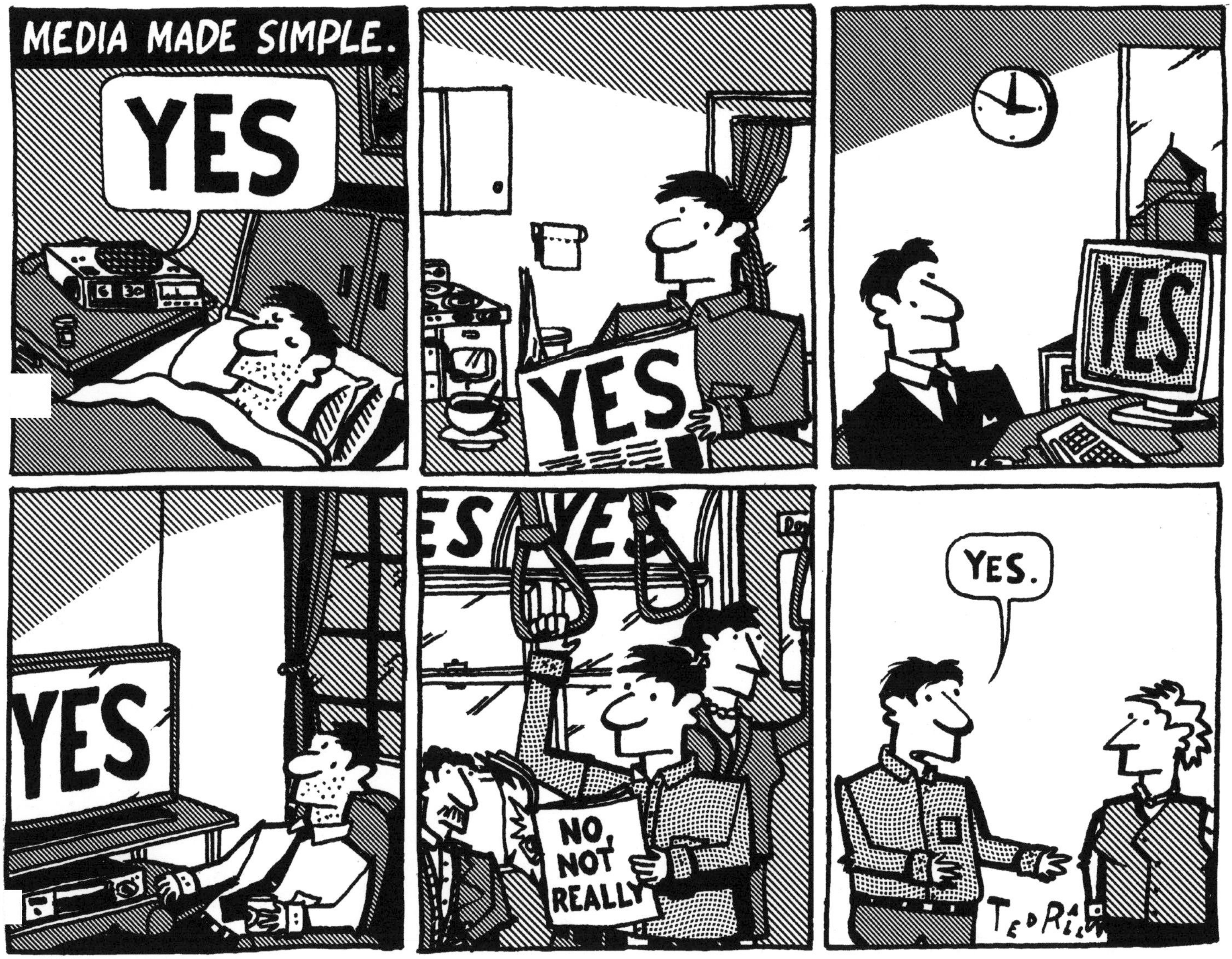
MEDIA MADE SIMPLE.
YES
YES
YES
YES
ES YES
NO, NOT REALLY
YES.
TED RALL

The '04 election campaign revived the issue of Bush's spotty service record of dodging the draft—er, keeping Texas safe during the Vietnam War.

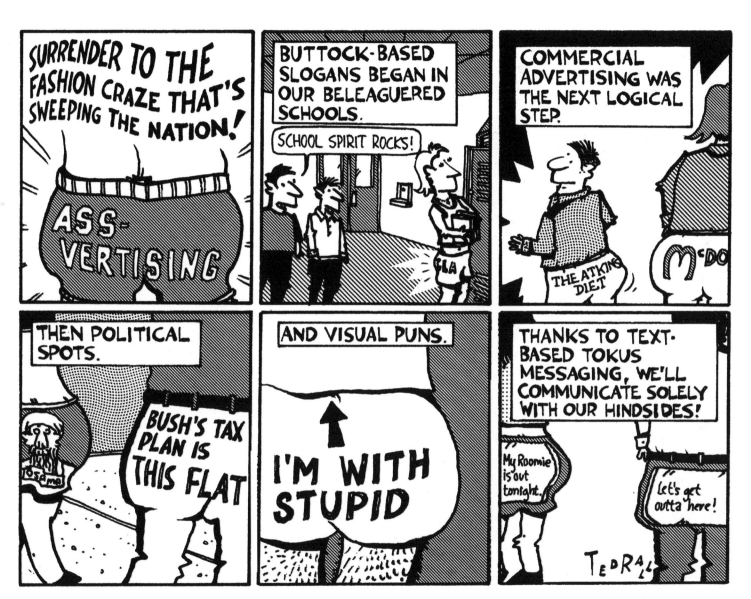

Names of schools began appearing on tuckuses in the nation's streets and malls.

Gay marriage became the "wedge issue" of 2004.

America killed one Al Qaeda number 2 after another.

Wounded veterans of the war in Iraq, lauded by the media, reminded me of those who had been similarly exploited and then abandoned after Vietnam.

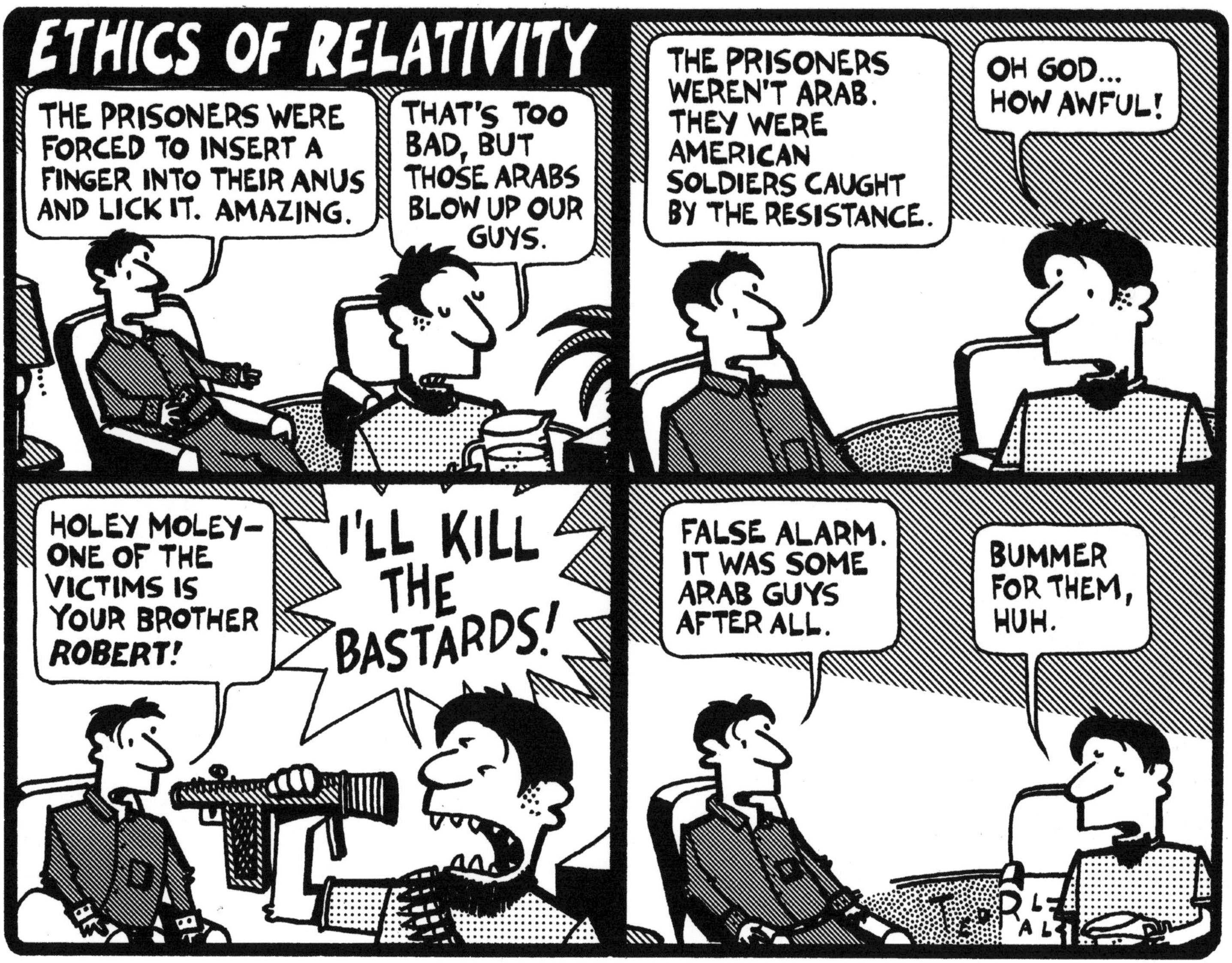
ETHICS OF RELATIVITY
THE PRISONERS WERE FORCED TO INSERT A FINGER INTO THEIR ANUS AND LICK IT. AMAZING.
THAT'S TOO BAD, BUT THOSE ARABS BLOW UP OUR GUYS.
THE PRISONERS WEREN'T ARAB. THEY WERE AMERICAN SOLDIERS CAUGHT BY THE RESISTANCE.
OH GOD... HOW AWFUL!
HOLEY MOLEY— ONE OF THE VICTIMS IS YOUR BROTHER ROBERT!
I'LL KILL THE BASTARDS!
FALSE ALARM. IT WAS SOME ARAB GUYS AFTER ALL.
BUMMER FOR THEM, HUH.
TED RALL

Those who commit overkill play into their opponents' hands by exposing themselves as monsters.

In a rare ploy, one of my fellow editorial cartoonists decided to attack me in one of his cartoons. I thought one-upping him would be even more "meta," and thus amusing.

FATHER-SON ADVICE

WHEN I WAS SINGLE, I DATED 3 WOMEN. ONE WAS SMART, ANOTHER FUN AND THE LAST SEXY.

IT SOUNDS BAD BUT IT WORKED OUT GREAT. I DIDN'T HAVE ENOUGH TIME FOR ANY OF THEM, SO THEY EACH WANTED ME MORE!

SO HOW'D YOU END UP GETTING MARRIED?

YOUR MOM WAS SCHIZO.

DATING AUTO-DESTRUCT

IT'S QUIET.

TOO QUIET.

I CAN'T LET HER TAKE THE INITIATIVE. I'M GONNA DUMP HER BEFORE—

TED?

I HATE YOU. YOU SUCK. GET OUT. NEVER CALL ME AGAIN.

DAMN!

I drew a series of cartoons about men, sex, and relationships for *Men's Health*. It was a welcome chance to get back to social commentary, a topic that the explosive post-9/11 world had made more difficult to justify.

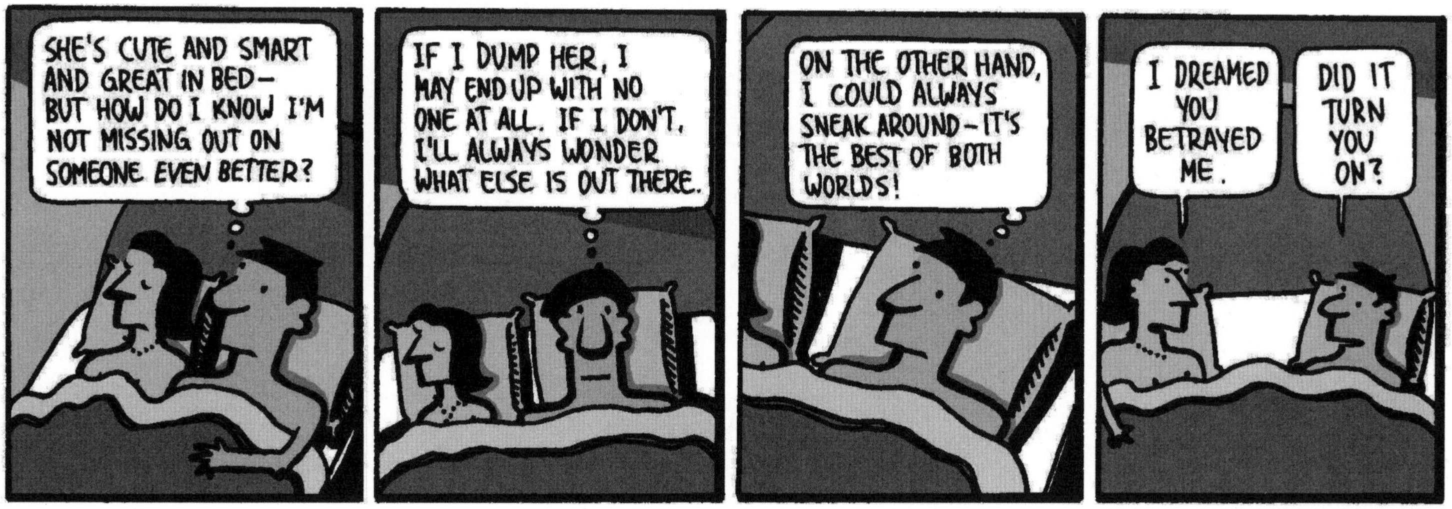
SHE'S CUTE AND SMART AND GREAT IN BED– BUT HOW DO I KNOW I'M NOT MISSING OUT ON SOMEONE *EVEN* BETTER?
IF I DUMP HER, I MAY END UP WITH NO ONE AT ALL. IF I DON'T, I'LL ALWAYS WONDER WHAT ELSE IS OUT THERE.
ON THE OTHER HAND, I COULD ALWAYS SNEAK AROUND – IT'S THE BEST OF BOTH WORLDS!
I DREAMED YOU BETRAYED ME.
DID IT TURN YOU ON?

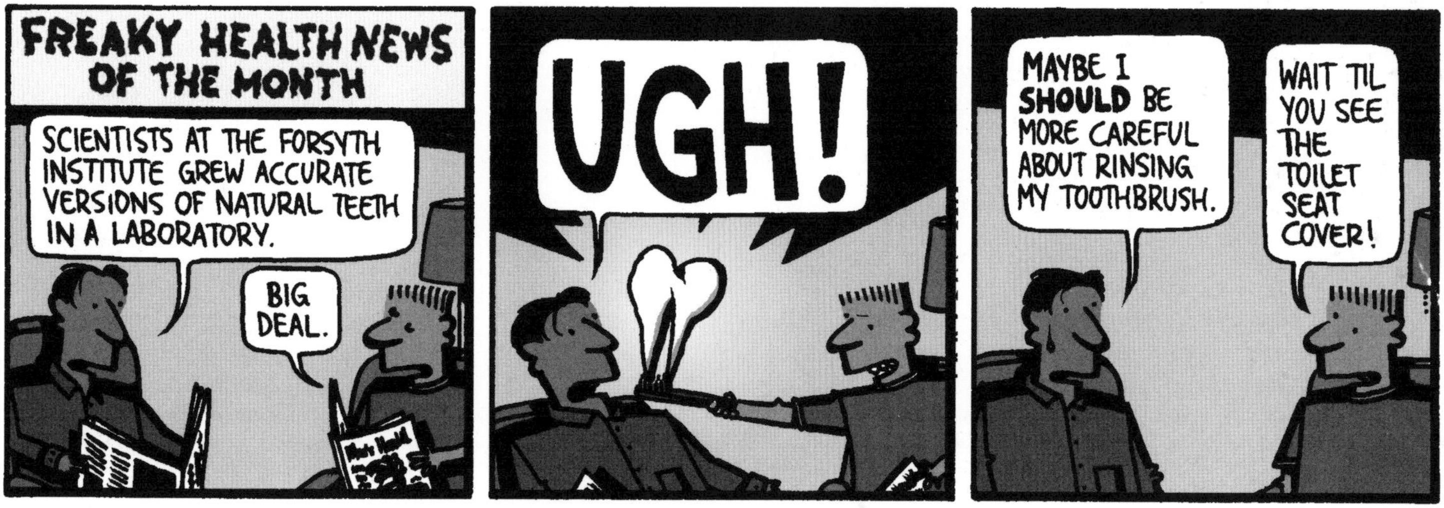
FREAKY HEALTH NEWS OF THE MONTH
SCIENTISTS AT THE FORSYTH INSTITUTE GREW ACCURATE VERSIONS OF NATURAL TEETH IN A LABORATORY.
BIG DEAL.
UGH!
MAYBE I **SHOULD** BE MORE CAREFUL ABOUT RINSING MY TOOTHBRUSH.
WAIT TIL YOU SEE THE TOILET SEAT COVER!

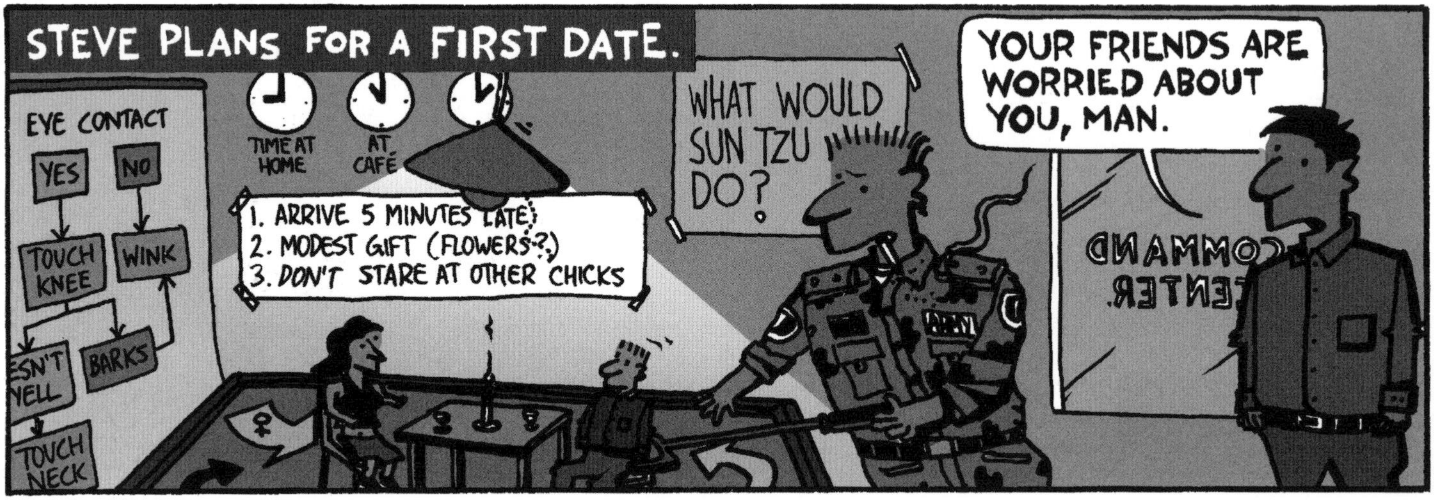
STEVE PLANS FOR A FIRST DATE.
EYE CONTACT
YES
NO
TOUCH KNEE
WINK
ESN'T YELL
BARKS
TOUCH NECK
TIME AT HOME
AT CAFÉ
1. ARRIVE 5 MINUTES LATE
2. MODEST GIFT (FLOWERS?)
3. DON'T STARE AT OTHER CHICKS
WHAT WOULD SUN TZU DO?
ARMY
YOUR FRIENDS ARE WORRIED ABOUT YOU, MAN.

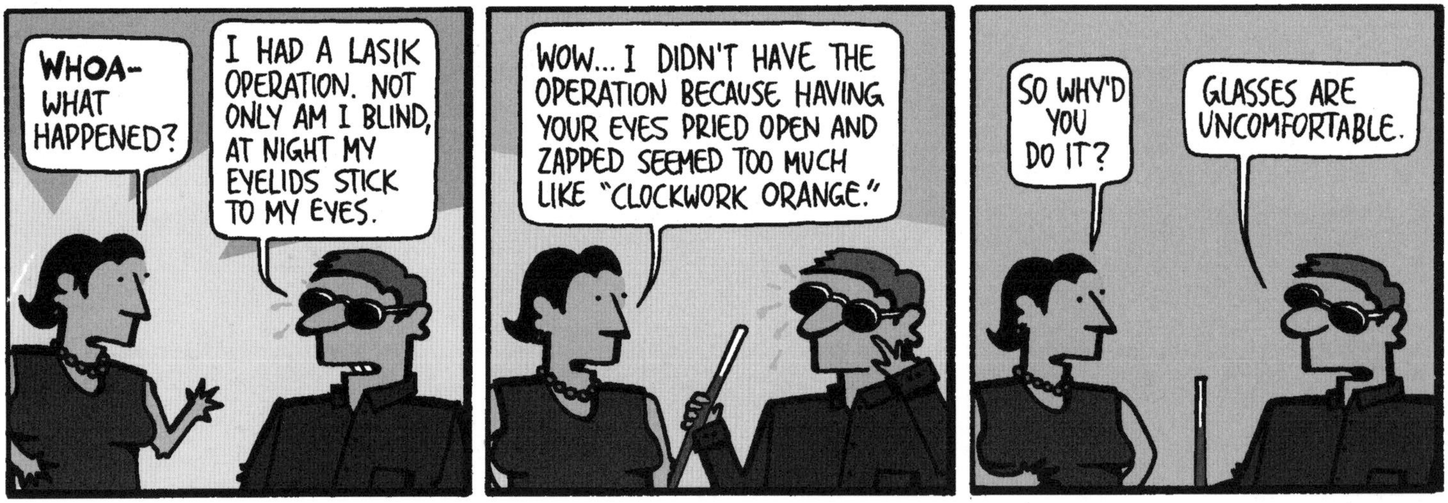
WHOA- WHAT HAPPENED?
I HAD A LASIK OPERATION. NOT ONLY AM I BLIND, AT NIGHT MY EYELIDS STICK TO MY EYES.
WOW... I DIDN'T HAVE THE OPERATION BECAUSE HAVING YOUR EYES PRIED OPEN AND ZAPPED SEEMED TOO MUCH LIKE "CLOCKWORK ORANGE."
SO WHY'D YOU DO IT?
GLASSES ARE UNCOMFORTABLE.

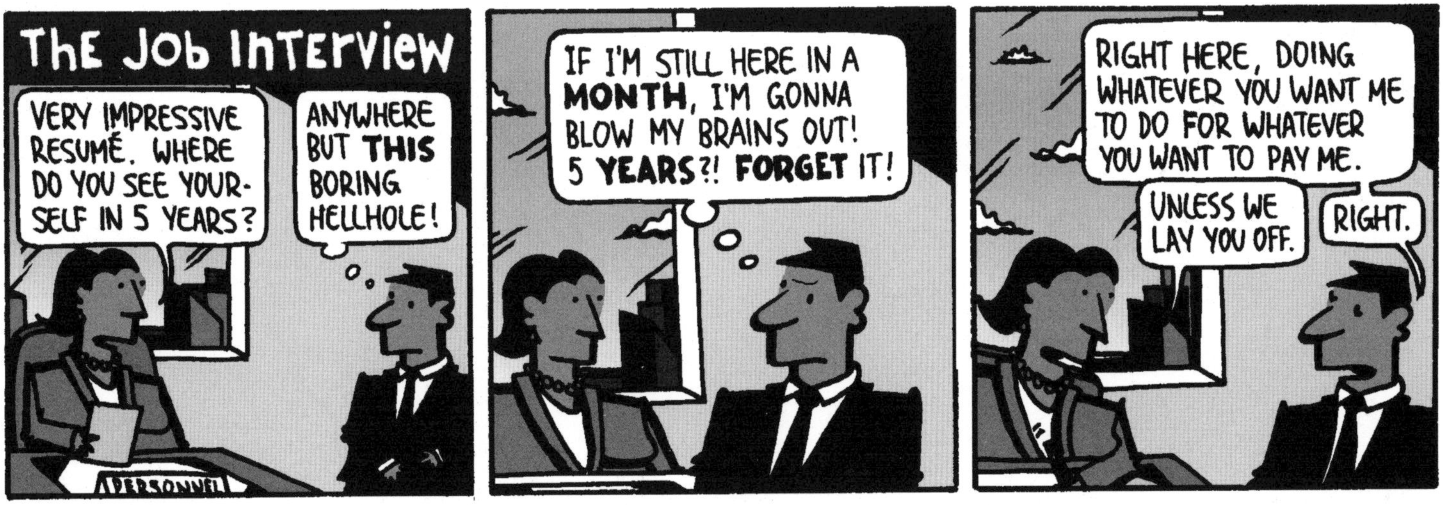
THE JOB INTERVIEW
VERY IMPRESSIVE RESUMÉ. WHERE DO YOU SEE YOURSELF IN 5 YEARS?
ANYWHERE BUT THIS BORING HELLHOLE!
IF I'M STILL HERE IN A MONTH, I'M GONNA BLOW MY BRAINS OUT! 5 YEARS?! FORGET IT!
RIGHT HERE, DOING WHATEVER YOU WANT ME TO DO FOR WHATEVER YOU WANT TO PAY ME.
UNLESS WE LAY YOU OFF.
RIGHT.

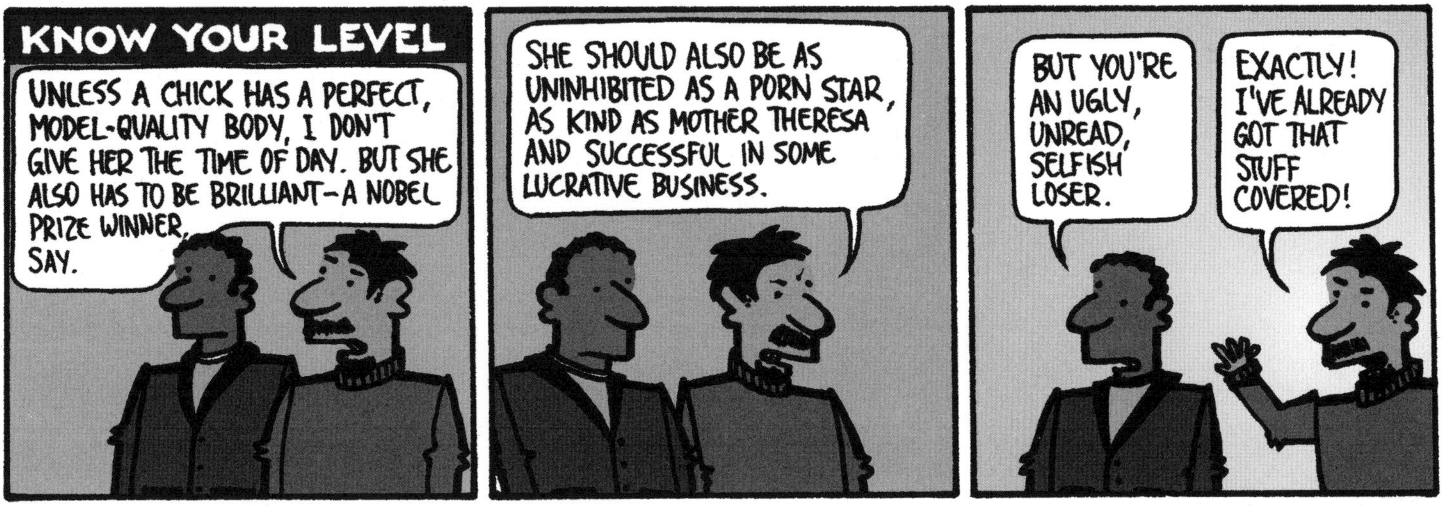
KNOW YOUR LEVEL
UNLESS A CHICK HAS A PERFECT, MODEL-QUALITY BODY, I DON'T GIVE HER THE TIME OF DAY. BUT SHE ALSO HAS TO BE BRILLIANT—A NOBEL PRIZE WINNER, SAY.
SHE SHOULD ALSO BE AS UNINHIBITED AS A PORN STAR, AS KIND AS MOTHER THERESA AND SUCCESSFUL IN SOME LUCRATIVE BUSINESS.
BUT YOU'RE AN UGLY, UNREAD, SELFISH LOSER.
EXACTLY! I'VE ALREADY GOT THAT STUFF COVERED!

I WASN'T RAISED TO END UP LIKE THIS. "REACH FOR THE STARS," MOM SAID.

I WAS A **WILD MAN**! GIRLS **LOVED** ME! LIFE WAS A FEEDING FRENZY AND I WAS A **GREAT WHITE**! I COULD—I WILL—BE A SHARK AGAIN!

OOOOH... LOOK AT THAT... 20% OFF SHIPPING ON AMAZON!

WHAT MAKES A MAN A MAN? SIMPLE: WHEN HE HAS VERY NEARLY DIED.

I'M A LOUSY DRIVER. I'VE TOTALLED 3 CARS AND A GIRL-FRIEND!

OF COURSE, NEAR-DEATH EXPERIENCES FOLLOW RECKLESSNESS. THE ROAD TO MANLINESS IS LITTERED WITH EMPTY BEER CANS.

I SPENT THE WEEKEND HUNTING FOR OSAMA IN YEMEN. YES: I WAS DRUNK.

SO: ARE YOU A REAL MAN?

I TRY TO AVOID DOING STUPID THINGS.

DON'T TALK TO ME, PANSY.

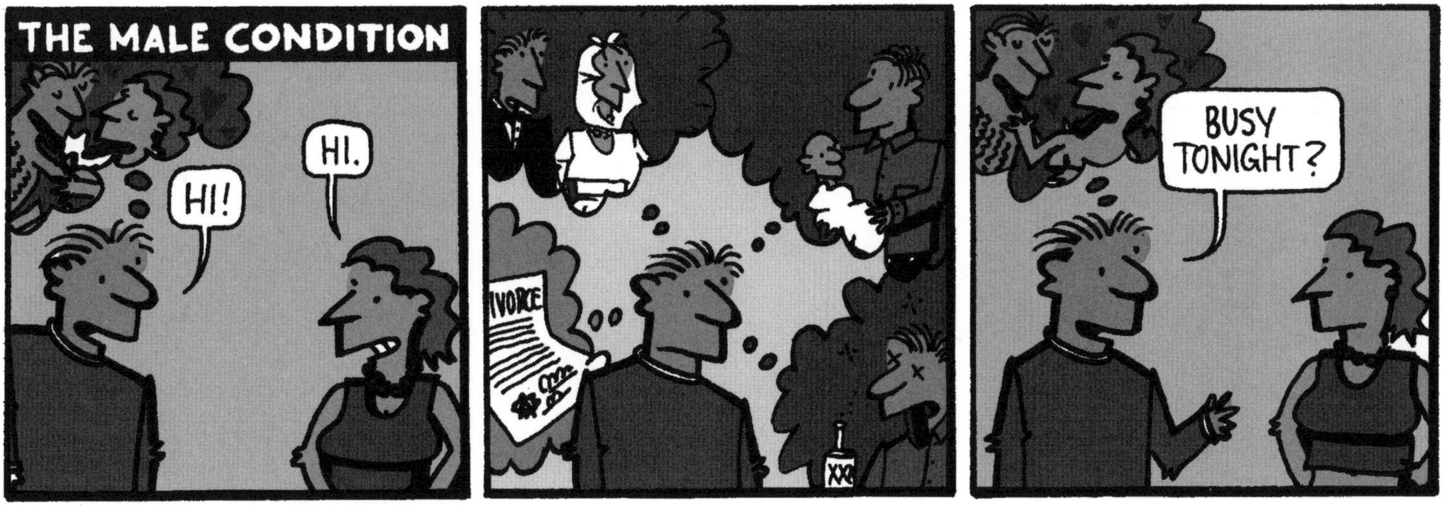
THE MALE CONDITION
HI!
HI.
IVORCE
BUSY TONIGHT?

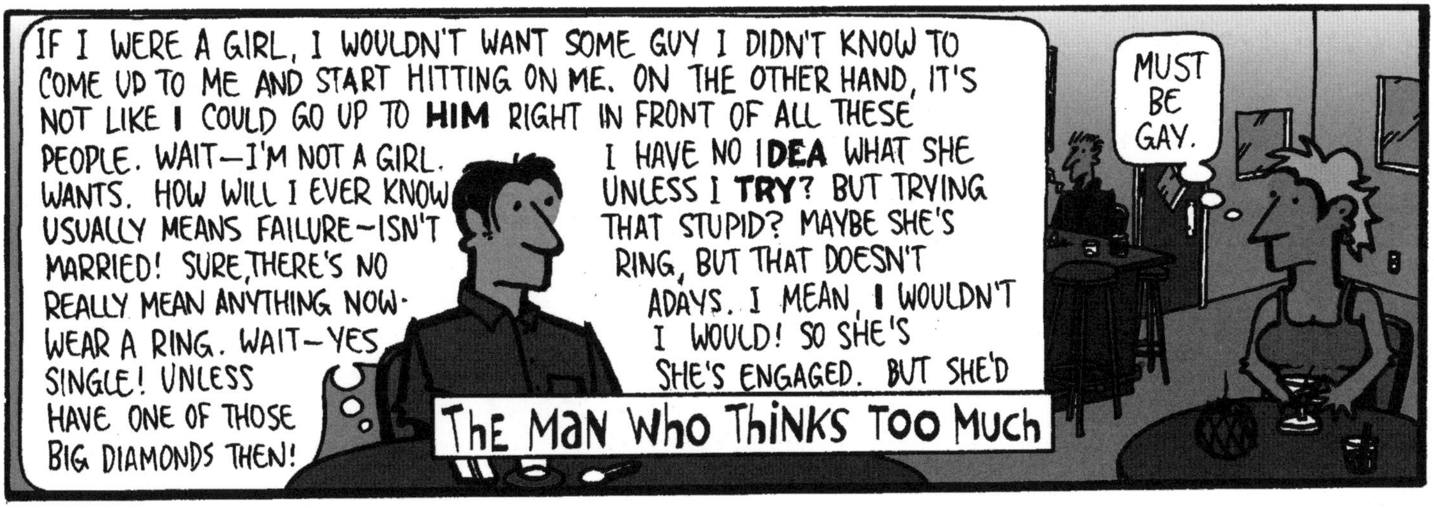
IF I WERE A GIRL, I WOULDN'T WANT SOME GUY I DIDN'T KNOW TO COME UP TO ME AND START HITTING ON ME. ON THE OTHER HAND, IT'S NOT LIKE I COULD GO UP TO HIM RIGHT IN FRONT OF ALL THESE PEOPLE. WAIT—I'M NOT A GIRL. I HAVE NO IDEA WHAT SHE WANTS. HOW WILL I EVER KNOW UNLESS I TRY? BUT TRYING USUALLY MEANS FAILURE—ISN'T THAT STUPID? MAYBE SHE'S MARRIED! SURE, THERE'S NO RING, BUT THAT DOESN'T REALLY MEAN ANYTHING NOWADAYS. I MEAN, I WOULDN'T WEAR A RING. WAIT—YES I WOULD! SO SHE'S SINGLE! UNLESS SHE'S ENGAGED. BUT SHE'D HAVE ONE OF THOSE BIG DIAMONDS THEN!
MUST BE GAY.
The Man Who Thinks Too Much

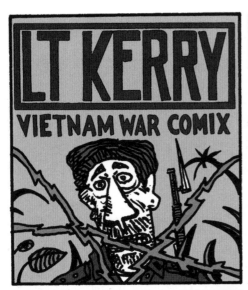

LT KERRY

VIETNAM WAR COMIX

THREE DECADES AFTER THE HORRORS OF JUNGLE WARFARE, THE HERO'S MEMORIES REMAIN FRESH.

MY FELLOW VETS CAN VERIFY THIS: I KICKED ASS IN 'NAM.

NO ONE BLASTED MORE GOOKS THAN I DID. WE RAPED 'EM, CUT OFF THEIR EARS AND ZAPPED THEIR GENITALS.

WE CAPTURED THOSE DIRTY SLOPES SO WE COULD CHOP OFF THEIR HEADS AND WATCH 'EM WIGGLE THEIR LIPS. IT WAS INCREDIBLE!

IF EVERY SOLDIER HAD BEEN AS WILLING AS ME TO NAPE ZIPPER-HEADS, WE WOULD HAVE **WON** THAT WAR!!!

WHAM WHAM WHAM

WHICH, OF COURSE, I WAS AGAINST.

TED RALL

The Democrats picked John Kerry, a Vietnam veteran who tried to balance his heroism with his subsequent opposition to the war, as their presidential nominee. The '04 campaign seemed like a replay of the debate of the '60s and '70s.

THE PERILS OF NUANCE

Kerry took the high road as Bush's attack dogs shredded him beyond recognition.

John McCain, the Arizona senator Bush had smeared as the father of an illegitimate daughter during the 2000 Republican primaries, endorsed Bush.

This cartoon, which appeared the day after Bush prevailed in the '04 election, depicts his win as the triumph of his pro-torture policy. (The gown became famous from photos of the Abu Ghraib torture scandal.)

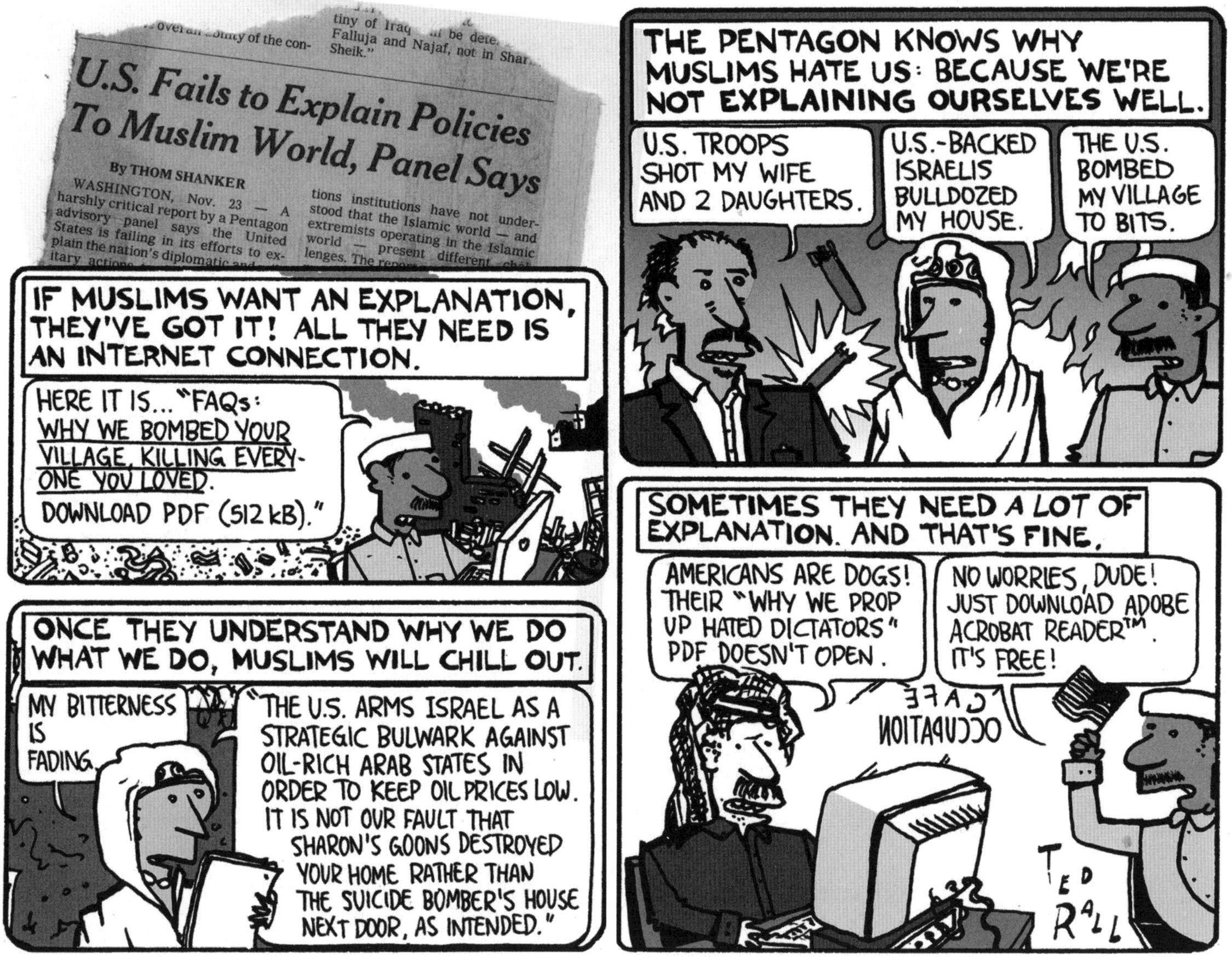
tiny of Iraq
Falluja and Najaf, not in
Sheik."
U.S. Fails to Explain Policies To Muslim World, Panel Says
By THOM SHANKER
WASHINGTON, Nov. 23 — A harshly critical report by a Pentagon advisory panel says the United States is failing in its efforts to explain the nation's diplomatic and
tions institutions have not understood that the Islamic world — and extremists operating in the Islamic world — present different
THE PENTAGON KNOWS WHY MUSLIMS HATE US: BECAUSE WE'RE NOT EXPLAINING OURSELVES WELL.
U.S. TROOPS SHOT MY WIFE AND 2 DAUGHTERS.
U.S.-BACKED ISRAELIS BULLDOZED MY HOUSE.
THE U.S. BOMBED MY VILLAGE TO BITS.
IF MUSLIMS WANT AN EXPLANATION, THEY'VE GOT IT! ALL THEY NEED IS AN INTERNET CONNECTION.
HERE IT IS... "FAQs: WHY WE BOMBED YOUR VILLAGE, KILLING EVERYONE YOU LOVED. DOWNLOAD PDF (512 kB)."
ONCE THEY UNDERSTAND WHY WE DO WHAT WE DO, MUSLIMS WILL CHILL OUT.
MY BITTERNESS IS FADING.
"THE U.S. ARMS ISRAEL AS A STRATEGIC BULWARK AGAINST OIL-RICH ARAB STATES IN ORDER TO KEEP OIL PRICES LOW. IT IS NOT OUR FAULT THAT SHARON'S GOONS DESTROYED YOUR HOME RATHER THAN THE SUICIDE BOMBER'S HOUSE NEXT DOOR, AS INTENDED."
SOMETIMES THEY NEED A LOT OF EXPLANATION. AND THAT'S FINE.
AMERICANS ARE DOGS! THEIR "WHY WE PROP UP HATED DICTATORS" PDF DOESN'T OPEN.
NO WORRIES, DUDE! JUST DOWNLOAD ADOBE ACROBAT READER™. IT'S FREE!
TED RALL

THE RESERVE BACKUP GUARD DEFENDS AMERICA WHEN EVERYONE ELSE IS TOO BUSY. WELL, THEY'RE BUSY. WHICH IS WHY

WE'RE LOOKING FOR A FEW SO-SO HOMBRES!

WE'RE THE NATION'S 4TH LINE OF DEFENSE. WHEN THE PRESIDENT RUNS OUT OF REGULAR ARMY, RESERVE AND NATIONAL GUARD TROOPS, HE CALLS US: THE RESERVE NATIONAL GUARD!

DO YOU HAVE WHAT IT TAKES?

CLEAN UNDER-WEAR

PROOF OF HETERO-SEXUALITY

OWN TRANSPORT-ATION

OUR PROMISE

WITH THE EXCEPTION OF THE FROST EMERGENCY OF 1911, THE U.S. RESERVE BACKUP GUARD HAS NEVER, EVER BEEN CALLED UP TO DO ANYTHING.

NO NEED TO READ THIS ↓

THE PRESIDENT RESERVES THE RIGHT TO CALL UP THE U.S. RESERVE BACKUP GUARD ANYTIME HE FEELS LIKE IT FOR ANY REASON WHATSOEVER. SHOULD YOU BE CALLED UP, YOU WILL GO WHEREVER WE SEND YOU, FOR ANY DUTY WE ORDER YOU TO PERFORM. WHEN YOUR TERM OF SERVICE EXPIRES, YOU WILL REMAIN ELIGIBLE FOR FURTHER SERVICE AS WE SEE FIT. SUCH SERVICE MAY INCLUDE BEING SENT TO ACTIVE WAR ZONES. YOU MAY BE SENT WITHOUT ADEQUATE TRAINING AND/OR EQUIPMENT. YOUR BENEFITS CAN BE REDUCED OR ELIMINATED WHENEVER WE FEEL LIKE IT, BUT SUCH A CHANGE DOES NOT REDUCE YOUR OBLIGATIONS, WHICH REMAIN PERPETUAL.

THE U.S. RESERVE BACKUP GUARD: WE DON'T ASK MUCH. ONE HOUR A MONTH. ONE WEEKEND PER YEAR. FREE HEALTHCARE.

The military relies increasingly on "weekend warriors" to fight its wars.

The impulse to send troops to disaster zones is a new and bizarre one.

Conservatives repeatedly argue that liberals have something against Christmas.
Liberals don't seem to know what they're talking about.

DISMAYED BY ANTI-AMERICANISM? IMPROVE OUR INTERNATIONAL REPUTATION BY

FUNDING GOOD DEEDS TO CANCEL EVILDOING!

EACH TIME THE MILITARY DELIVERS AID TO A DISASTER ZONE...

...IT GETS A FREE PASS FOR A WAR!

EVERY POLITICAL PRISONER WE LIBERATE...

...GETS US OFF THE HOOK FOR TORTURING ONE OF OURS!

THE U.N. CONDEMNS THIS ILLEGAL INV— WAIT A SEC. THE U.S. IS USING A FREE WAR CREDIT.

WAR CREDIT

BEST OF ALL...

BUILDING A SCHOOL FOR AFGHAN GIRLS...

...NULLIFIES TAKING OUT AN AFGHAN WEDDING PARTY!

EVERY ETHNIC MEAL YOU EAT... HERE

...ALLOWS AN AMERICAN TOURIST TO ACT LIKE A PIG OVERSEAS!

YOU SPEEK INGLISH, BOY?!!

TEDRALL

MORAL EQUIVALENCE: EVERY LIFE WE SAVE BUYS US THE RIGHT TO ONE FREE MURDER!

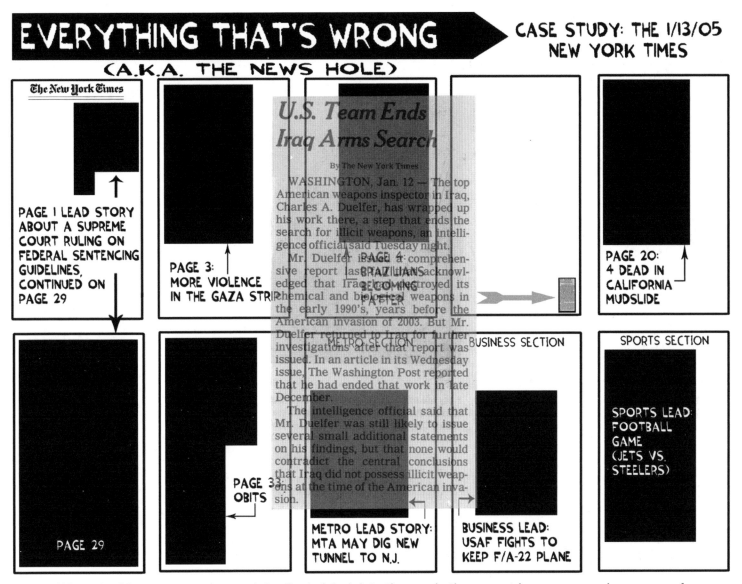

EVERYTHING THAT'S WRONG

(A.K.A. THE NEWS HOLE)

The New York Times

PAGE 1 LEAD STORY ABOUT A SUPREME COURT RULING ON FEDERAL SENTENCING GUIDELINES, CONTINUED ON PAGE 29

PAGE 3: MORE VIOLENCE IN THE GAZA STRIP

PAGE 29

PAGE 33 OBITS

METRO SECTION

METRO LEAD STORY: MTA MAY DIG NEW TUNNEL TO N.J.

U.S. Team Ends Iraq Arms Search

By The New York Times

WASHINGTON, Jan. 12 — The top American weapons inspector in Iraq, Charles A. Duelfer, has wrapped up his work there, a step that ends the search for illicit weapons, an intelligence official said Tuesday night.

Mr. Duelfer issued a comprehensive report last fall that acknowledged that Iraq destroyed its chemical and biological weapons in the early 1990's, years before the American invasion of 2003. But Mr. Duelfer returned to Iraq for further investigations after that report was issued. In an article in its Wednesday issue, The Washington Post reported that he had ended that work in late December.

The intelligence official said that Mr. Duelfer was still likely to issue several small additional statements on his findings, but that none would contradict the central conclusions that Iraq did not possess illicit weapons at the time of the American invasion.

PAGE 4: BRAZILIANS BECOMING DIETER

BUSINESS SECTION

BUSINESS LEAD: USAF FIGHTS TO KEEP F/A-22 PLANE

PAGE 20: 4 DEAD IN CALIFORNIA MUDSLIDE

SPORTS SECTION

SPORTS LEAD: FOOTBALL GAME (JETS VS. STEELERS)

When the biggest controversy of the Bush Administration—whether or not Iraq possessed weapons of mass destruction—was settled, the *New York Times* and other papers ran the news as a tiny piece buried deep inside the paper.

I like to draw parallels between government policy and personal politics.

man BiTES GOD

DO YOU BELIEVE IN GOD, MY UBIQUITOUS AND OMNISCIENT FATHER?

YOU BET!

INRI

LYING SACK OF CORPORATE TOXIC WASTE! IF YOU REALLY BELIEVED YOU WOULD FACE ETERNAL JUDGMENT BASED ON YOUR GOOD AND BAD DEEDS—*BELIEVED* IT LIKE YOU BELIEVE THE SKY IS BLUE—YOU'D BEHAVE 100% DIFFERENTLY!

DUDE! NOW I'M A PERCH.

ZAP!

LOOK AT THAT WINO. IF YOU WERE AT *ALL* CONCERNED ABOUT BURNING IN HELL *FOREVER*, YOU'D INVITE HIM HOME! YOU'D FIGHT OFF OTHER DO-GOODERS FOR A CHANCE AT HIM!

JESUS DUDE, **NO ONE** DOES THAT.

EXACTLY! I SWEAR—SOMETIMES IT'S LIKE I DON'T EVEN—

EXIST? HEY, I'M NO LONGER A PERCH.

TEDRALL

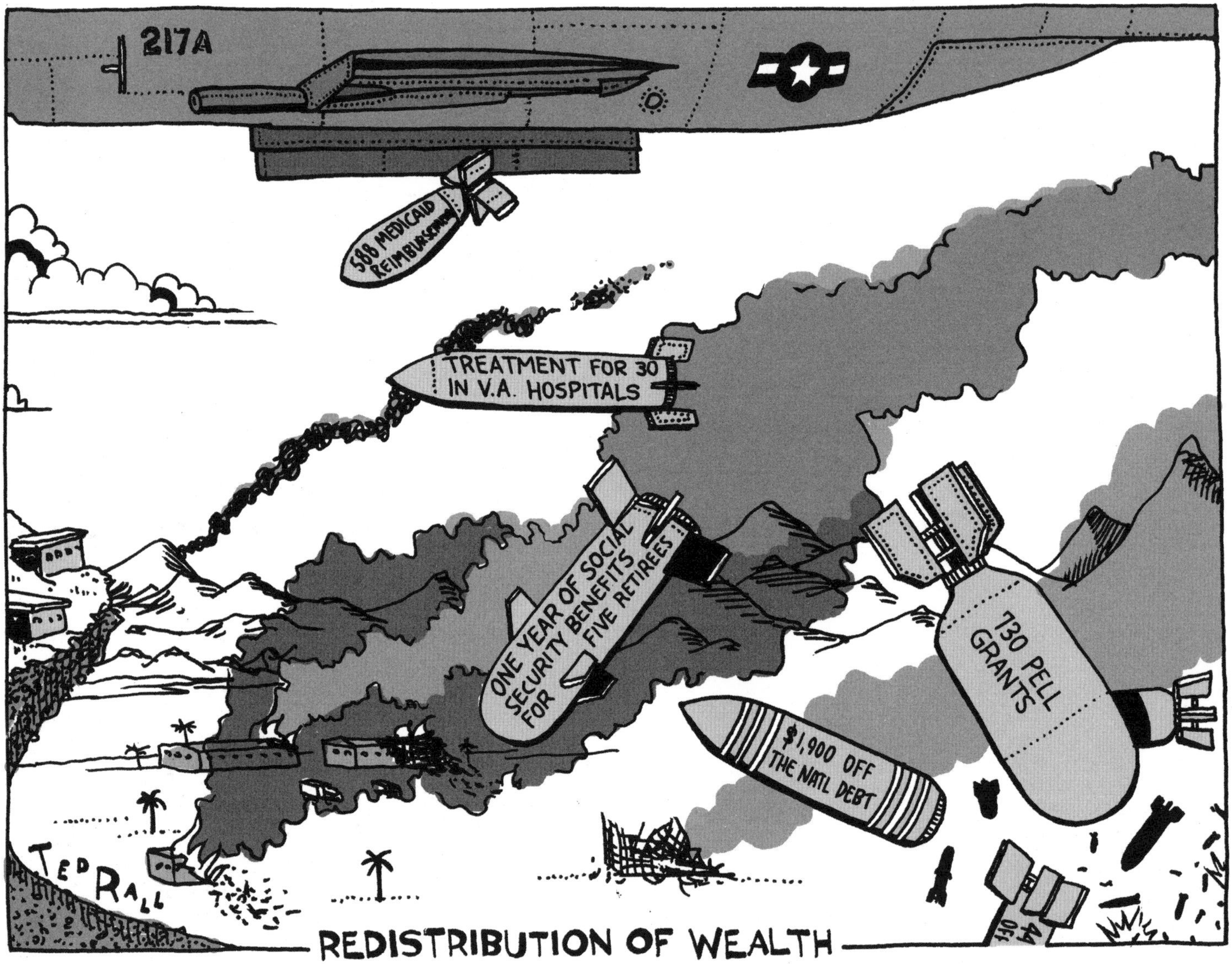
217A
588 MEDICAID
TREATMENT FOR 30 IN V.A. HOSPITALS
ONE YEAR OF SOCIAL SECURITY BENEFITS FOR FIVE RETIREES
730 PELL GRANTS
$1,900 OFF THE NATL DEBT
TED RALL
REDISTRIBUTION OF WEALTH

Bush's critics compared him to Hitler, enraging conservatives.

I tried to keep the Administration's assertion that it's OK to torture prisoners alive in the media.

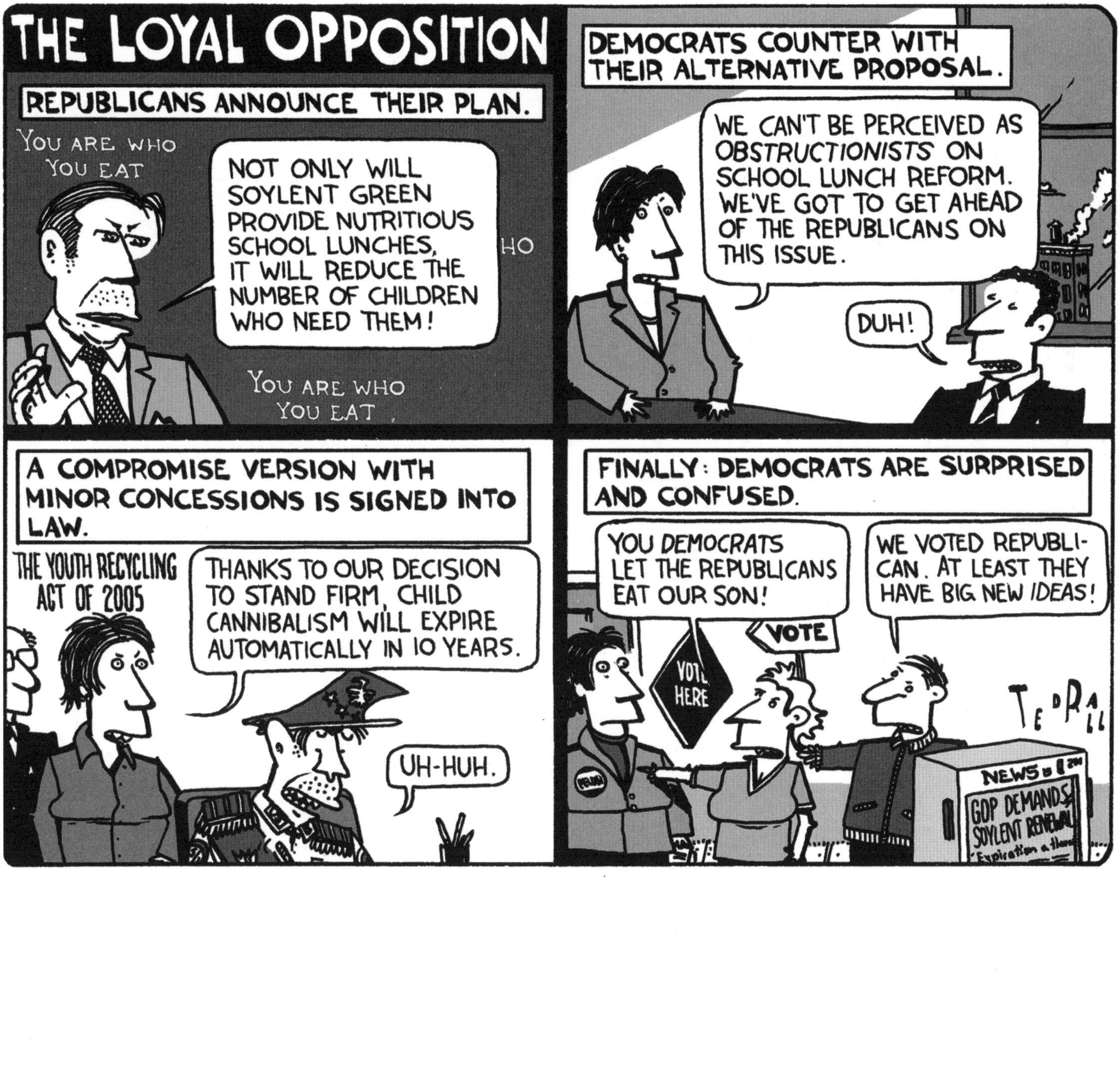
THE LOYAL OPPOSITION
REPUBLICANS ANNOUNCE THEIR PLAN.
YOU ARE WHO YOU EAT
NOT ONLY WILL SOYLENT GREEN PROVIDE NUTRITIOUS SCHOOL LUNCHES, IT WILL REDUCE THE NUMBER OF CHILDREN WHO NEED THEM!
YOU ARE WHO YOU EAT
DEMOCRATS COUNTER WITH THEIR ALTERNATIVE PROPOSAL.
WE CAN'T BE PERCEIVED AS OBSTRUCTIONISTS ON SCHOOL LUNCH REFORM. WE'VE GOT TO GET AHEAD OF THE REPUBLICANS ON THIS ISSUE.
DUH!
A COMPROMISE VERSION WITH MINOR CONCESSIONS IS SIGNED INTO LAW.
THE YOUTH RECYCLING ACT OF 2005
THANKS TO OUR DECISION TO STAND FIRM, CHILD CANNIBALISM WILL EXPIRE AUTOMATICALLY IN 10 YEARS.
UH-HUH.
FINALLY: DEMOCRATS ARE SURPRISED AND CONFUSED.
YOU DEMOCRATS LET THE REPUBLICANS EAT OUR SON!
WE VOTED REPUBLICAN. AT LEAST THEY HAVE BIG NEW IDEAS!
VOTE
VOTE HERE
TED RALL
NEWS
GOP DEMANDS SOYLENT RENEWAL

What is it like to be a religious minority in your own country? Although I picked an obscure religion to make the point, a few Zoroastrians wrote to express approval.

Ronald Reagan and Pope John Paul II, both credited with ending Communism in the Eastern bloc, died nearly at the same time.

7 Periods is a regular comic strip appearing in *Mad* magazine about the formative experience of high school.

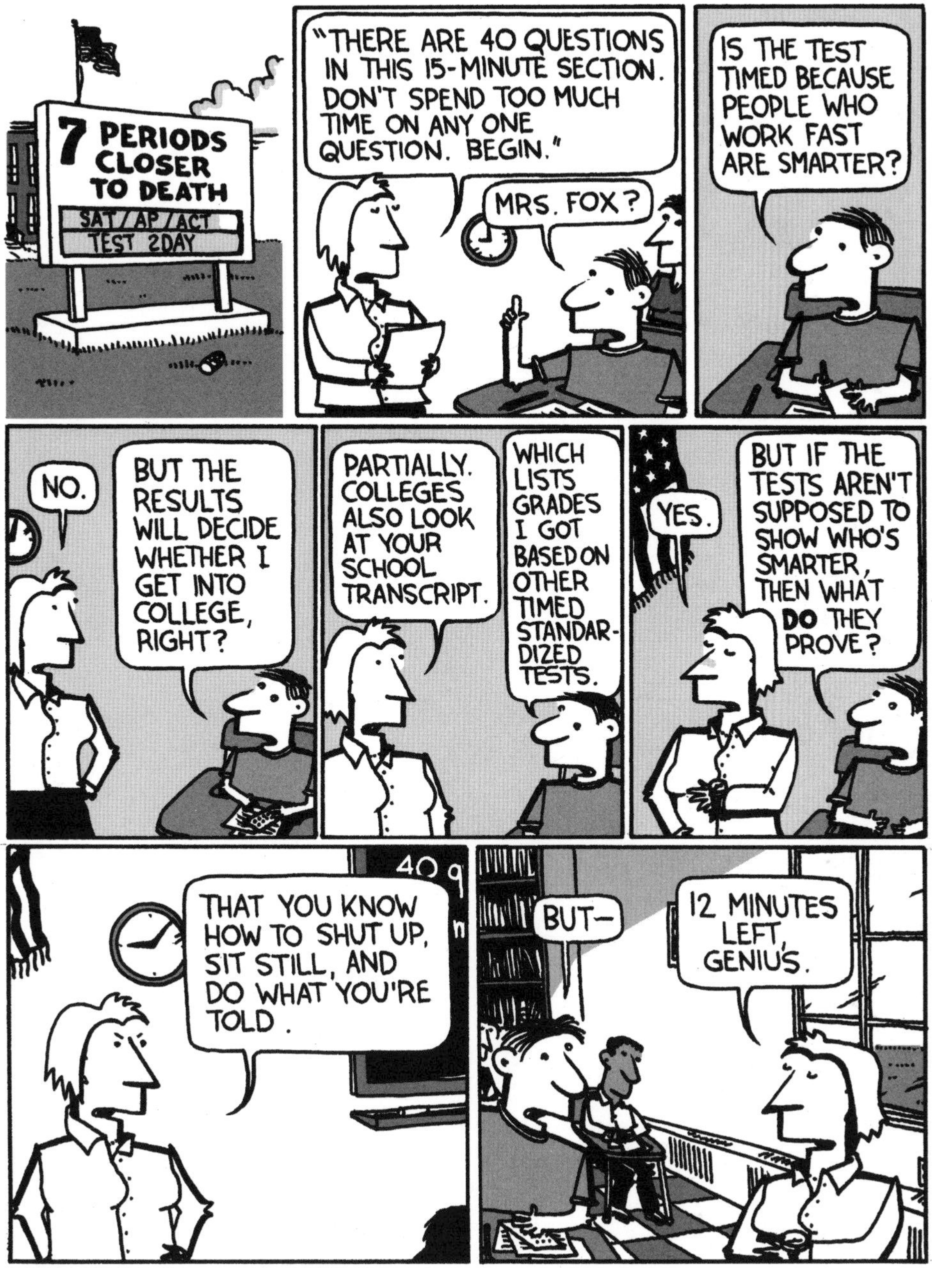
7 PERIODS CLOSER TO DEATH
SAT/AP/ACT TEST 2DAY
"THERE ARE 40 QUESTIONS IN THIS 15-MINUTE SECTION. DON'T SPEND TOO MUCH TIME ON ANY ONE QUESTION. BEGIN."
MRS. FOX?
IS THE TEST TIMED BECAUSE PEOPLE WHO WORK FAST ARE SMARTER?
NO.
BUT THE RESULTS WILL DECIDE WHETHER I GET INTO COLLEGE, RIGHT?
PARTIALLY. COLLEGES ALSO LOOK AT YOUR SCHOOL TRANSCRIPT.
WHICH LISTS GRADES I GOT BASED ON OTHER TIMED STANDARDIZED TESTS.
YES.
BUT IF THE TESTS AREN'T SUPPOSED TO SHOW WHO'S SMARTER, THEN WHAT DO THEY PROVE?
THAT YOU KNOW HOW TO SHUT UP, SIT STILL, AND DO WHAT YOU'RE TOLD.
BUT—
12 MINUTES LEFT, GENIUS.

Fantabulaman, my other strip for *Mad*, is a postmodern parody of the superhero genre wherein the hero truly is, as advertised, so undefeatable as to be free of drama.

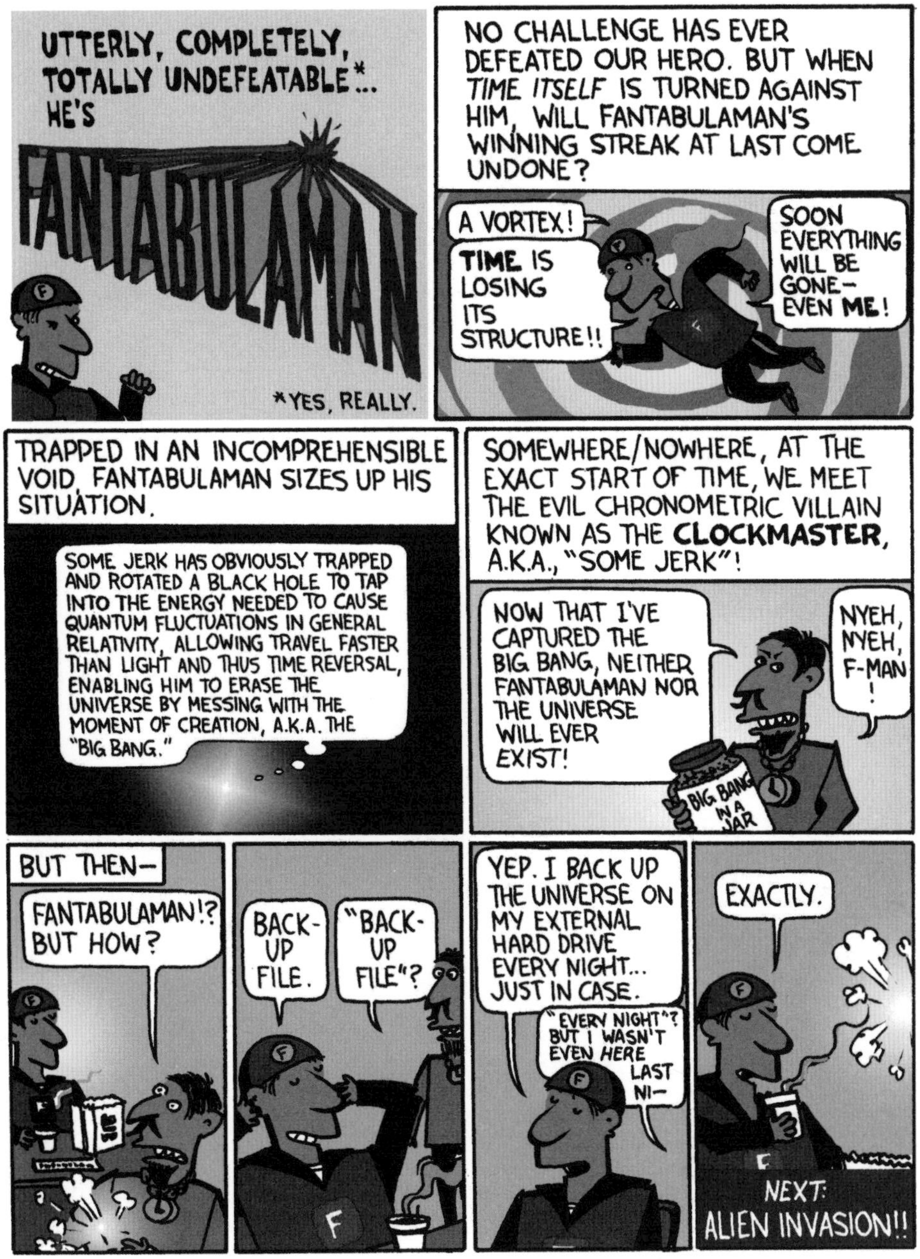
UTTERLY, COMPLETELY, TOTALLY UNDEFEATABLE*... HE'S
FANTABULAMAN
*YES, REALLY.
NO CHALLENGE HAS EVER DEFEATED OUR HERO. BUT WHEN TIME ITSELF IS TURNED AGAINST HIM, WILL FANTABULAMAN'S WINNING STREAK AT LAST COME UNDONE?
A VORTEX!
TIME IS LOSING ITS STRUCTURE!!
SOON EVERYTHING WILL BE GONE— EVEN ME!
TRAPPED IN AN INCOMPREHENSIBLE VOID, FANTABULAMAN SIZES UP HIS SITUATION.
SOME JERK HAS OBVIOUSLY TRAPPED AND ROTATED A BLACK HOLE TO TAP INTO THE ENERGY NEEDED TO CAUSE QUANTUM FLUCTUATIONS IN GENERAL RELATIVITY, ALLOWING TRAVEL FASTER THAN LIGHT AND THUS TIME REVERSAL, ENABLING HIM TO ERASE THE UNIVERSE BY MESSING WITH THE MOMENT OF CREATION, A.K.A. THE "BIG BANG."
SOMEWHERE/NOWHERE, AT THE EXACT START OF TIME, WE MEET THE EVIL CHRONOMETRIC VILLAIN KNOWN AS THE CLOCKMASTER, A.K.A., "SOME JERK"!
NOW THAT I'VE CAPTURED THE BIG BANG, NEITHER FANTABULAMAN NOR THE UNIVERSE WILL EVER EXIST!
NYEH, NYEH, F-MAN!
BIG BANG IN A JAR
BUT THEN—
FANTABULAMAN!? BUT HOW?
BACK-UP FILE.
"BACK-UP FILE"?
YEP. I BACK UP THE UNIVERSE ON MY EXTERNAL HARD DRIVE EVERY NIGHT... JUST IN CASE.
"EVERY NIGHT"? BUT I WASN'T EVEN HERE LAST NI—
EXACTLY.
NEXT: ALIEN INVASION!!

The media's role has shifted from reportage to stenography, a development placed in sharp relief by press scandals such as the storm surrounding *New York Times* writer Judith Miller, who served as an unofficial Bush mouthpiece during the run-up to the invasion of Iraq.

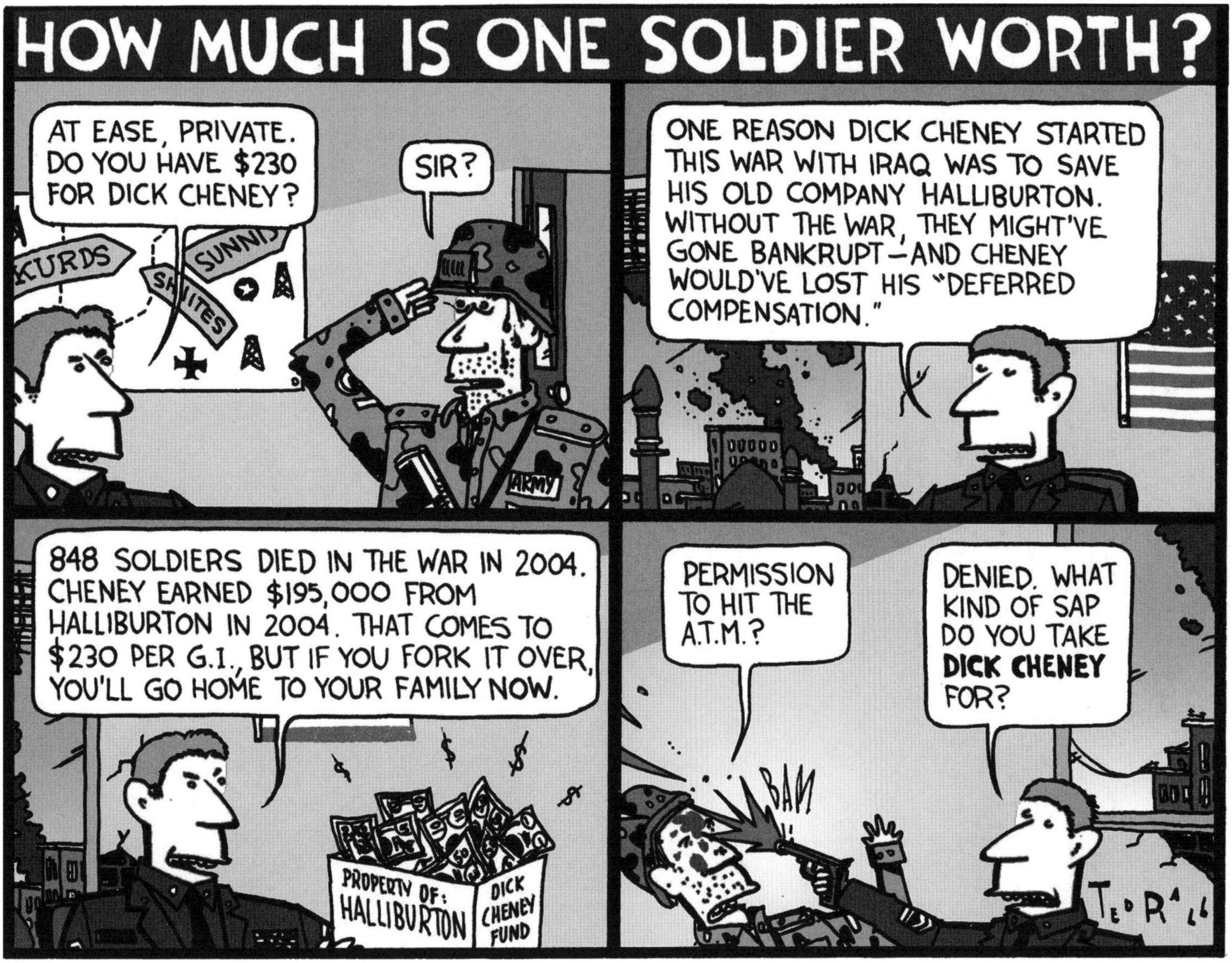
HOW MUCH IS ONE SOLDIER WORTH?
AT EASE, PRIVATE. DO YOU HAVE $230 FOR DICK CHENEY?
SIR?
KURDS
SUNNIS
SHIITES
ARMY
ONE REASON DICK CHENEY STARTED THIS WAR WITH IRAQ WAS TO SAVE HIS OLD COMPANY HALLIBURTON. WITHOUT THE WAR, THEY MIGHT'VE GONE BANKRUPT—AND CHENEY WOULD'VE LOST HIS "DEFERRED COMPENSATION."
848 SOLDIERS DIED IN THE WAR IN 2004. CHENEY EARNED $195,000 FROM HALLIBURTON IN 2004. THAT COMES TO $230 PER G.I., BUT IF YOU FORK IT OVER, YOU'LL GO HOME TO YOUR FAMILY NOW.
PROPERTY OF: HALLIBURTON
DICK CHENEY FUND
PERMISSION TO HIT THE A.T.M.?
DENIED. WHAT KIND OF SAP DO YOU TAKE **DICK CHENEY** FOR?
BAM
TED RALL

LIBERAL AND CONSERVATIVE SOLUTIONS TO PROBLEMS

SOARING REAL ESTATE PRICES PUT THE DREAM OF HOME OWNERSHIP OUT OF REACH OF YOUNG AMERICANS.

THE LIBERAL SOLUTION:

OUR PILOT PROGRAM WILL PROVIDE AFFORDABLE HOUSING FOR 38 INNER-CITY FAMILIES! WOO-HOO.

THE CONSERVATIVE SOLUTION:

FAGS. MEN HAVING GODLESS APE SEX WITH OTHER MEN. THEY MUST BE STOPPED!!!

PEOPLE CAN'T AFFORD DOCTORS' VISITS OR MEDICATIONS WHEN THEY GET SICK.

THE LIBERAL SOLUTION:

WELCOME TO THE 403RD DAY OF OUR BLUE-RIBBON INVESTIGATIVE COMMITTEE PANEL ON HEALTHCARE IN WHICH A MOTION YIELDING TIME TO THE DISTINGUISHED REPRESENTATIVE IS STILL PENDING.

THE CONSERVATIVE SOLUTION:

WHY DON'T THEY ALLOW PRAYER IN THE SCHOOLS? BECAUSE TEACHERS HATE GOD.

GLOBALIZATION IS MAKING IT HARDER TO FIND A GOOD JOB.

THE LIBERAL SOLUTION:

BOYCOTT WAL-MART

ALSO STARBUCKS

THE CONSERVATIVE SOLUTION:

YES. WE *WILL* TAKE OUR FIGHT TO POST THE TEN COMMANDMENTS IN COURTROOMS ALL THE WAY TO THE U.S. SUPREME COURT.

GAS PRICES KEEP RISING TO NEW HIGHS.

THE LIBERAL SOLUTION:

I'VE PROPOSED A LOW-INCOME GAS TAX REBATE BILL THAT WILL NEVER EVEN GET VOTED UPON.

WHY? BECAUSE THAT'S THE KIND OF DEMOCRATIC WILD MAN I AM.

SENATOR PARK

THE CONSERVATIVE SOLUTION:

AND NOW THEY WANNA GET **MARRIED!?** @★∅#! CORNHOLING **FAGS**!!!

Inspired by Al Pacino's line in *The Devil's Advocate* that God is an absentee landlord.

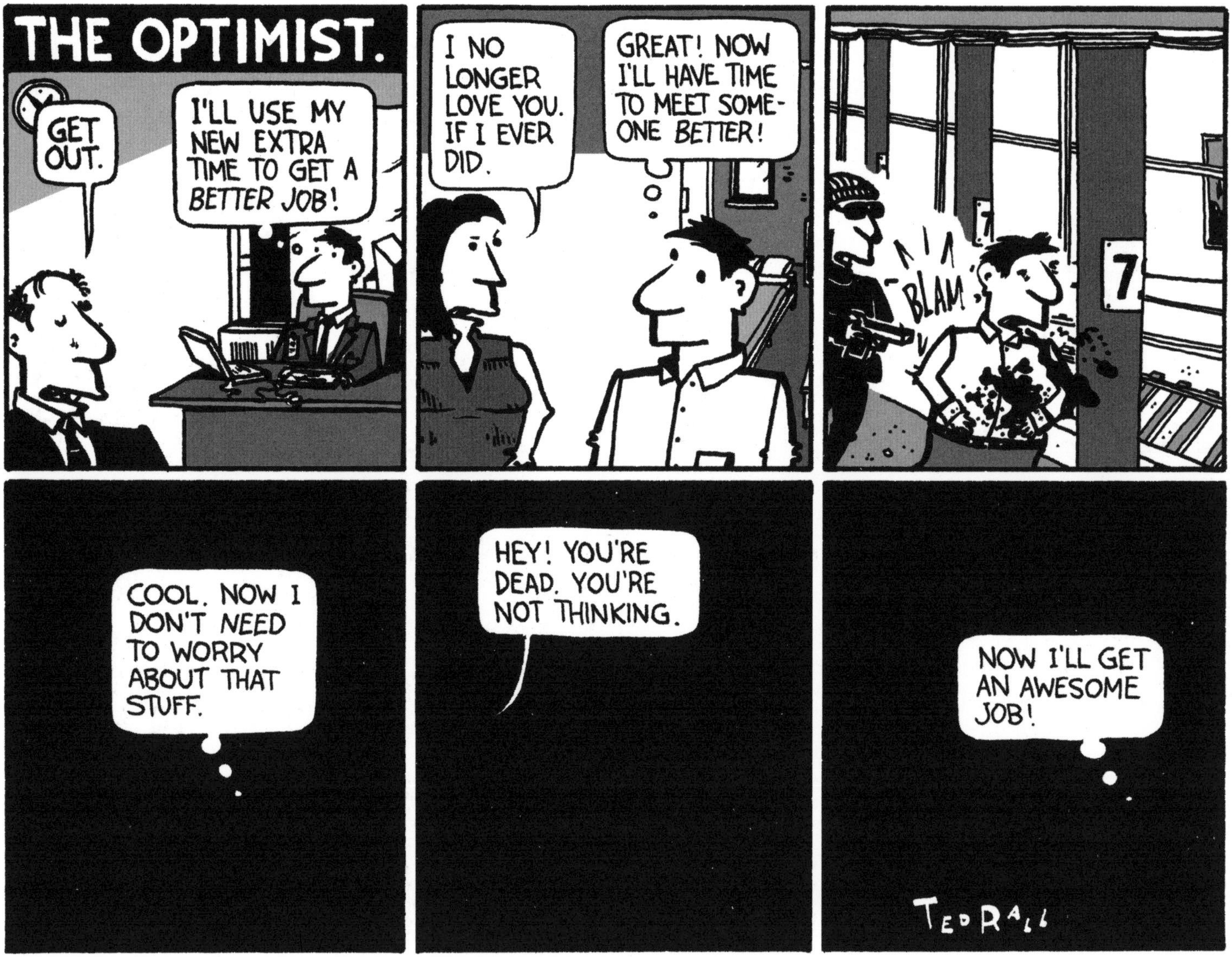
THE OPTIMIST.
GET OUT.
I'LL USE MY NEW EXTRA TIME TO GET A BETTER JOB!
I NO LONGER LOVE YOU. IF I EVER DID.
GREAT! NOW I'LL HAVE TIME TO MEET SOME-ONE BETTER!
7
BLAM!
7
COOL. NOW I DON'T NEED TO WORRY ABOUT THAT STUFF.
HEY! YOU'RE DEAD. YOU'RE NOT THINKING.
NOW I'LL GET AN AWESOME JOB!
TED RALL

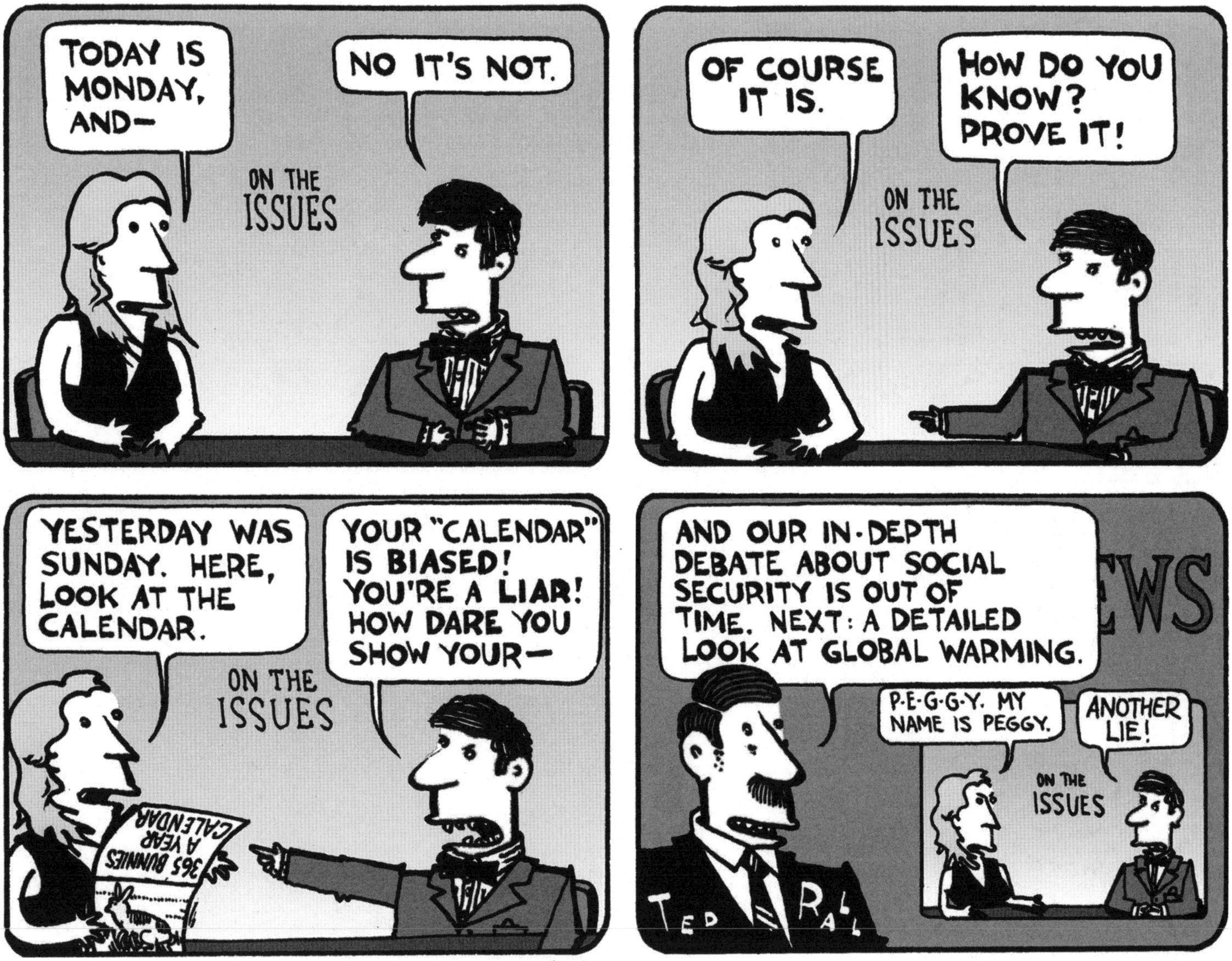
TODAY IS MONDAY, AND—
NO IT'S NOT.
ON THE ISSUES
OF COURSE IT IS.
HOW DO YOU KNOW? PROVE IT!
ON THE ISSUES
YESTERDAY WAS SUNDAY. HERE, LOOK AT THE CALENDAR.
YOUR "CALENDAR" IS BIASED! YOU'RE A LIAR! HOW DARE YOU SHOW YOUR—
ON THE ISSUES
365 BUNNIES A YEAR CALENDAR
AND OUR IN-DEPTH DEBATE ABOUT SOCIAL SECURITY IS OUT OF TIME. NEXT: A DETAILED LOOK AT GLOBAL WARMING.
P-E-G-G-Y. MY NAME IS PEGGY.
ANOTHER LIE!
ON THE ISSUES
TED RALL

Democrats are told that they can win more elections by sucking up to an increasingly ignorant electorate.

Republicans can't be reasoned with, but you have to admire their panache.

HOW THE FLAG-BURNING AMENDMENT WILL HELP

If the American flag is *really* sacred . . .

School prayer, another "wedge issue," continues to spark angry debate.

It's a perverse assertion: Why try to be liked by people who hate us because we've never tried to make them like us?

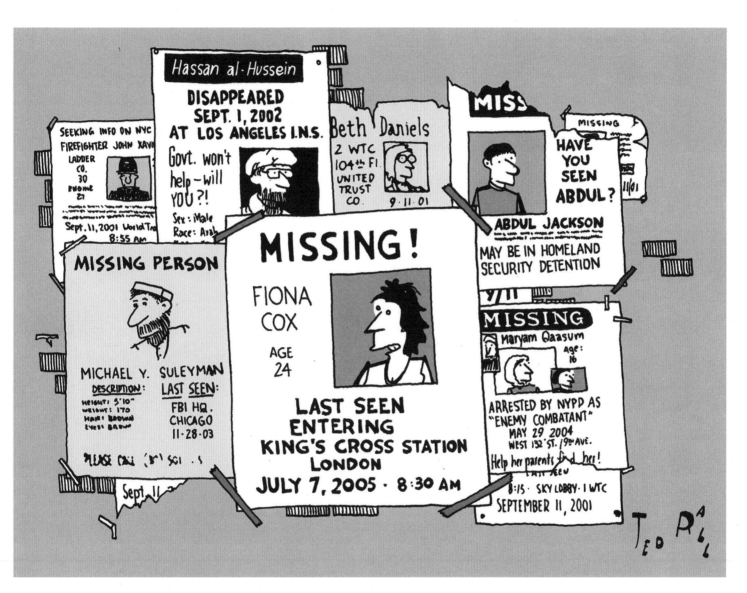

Missing persons posters sprang up after terrorist bombings in Madrid and London, reminding me that many people have gone "missing" since 9/11.

Inspired by "pollution credits," which allow corporations to pollute more by buying chits from those that pollute less.

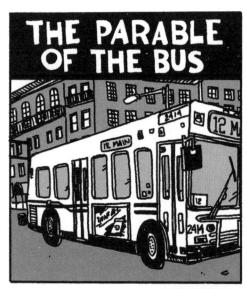

An analogy to the war in Iraq. After all, we've already invested so much blood and treasure—we have to spend more or it will all have been a waste!

The United States could seal its border if it made the slightest effort to do so.

Grumpy Americans criticized residents of New Orleans for having the nerve to live in a hurricane zone after Hurricane Katrina ravaged the city.

Cindy Sheehan, the mother of a GI killed in Iraq, stood vigil outside Bush's ranch in Crawford, Texas.

Liberals watched one scandal after another envelop the Bush Administration.

The vice president terrified even his supporters.

Inspired by the Werner Herzog documentary *Grizzly Man,* about a man who lived among ferocious bears before (predictably) being killed.

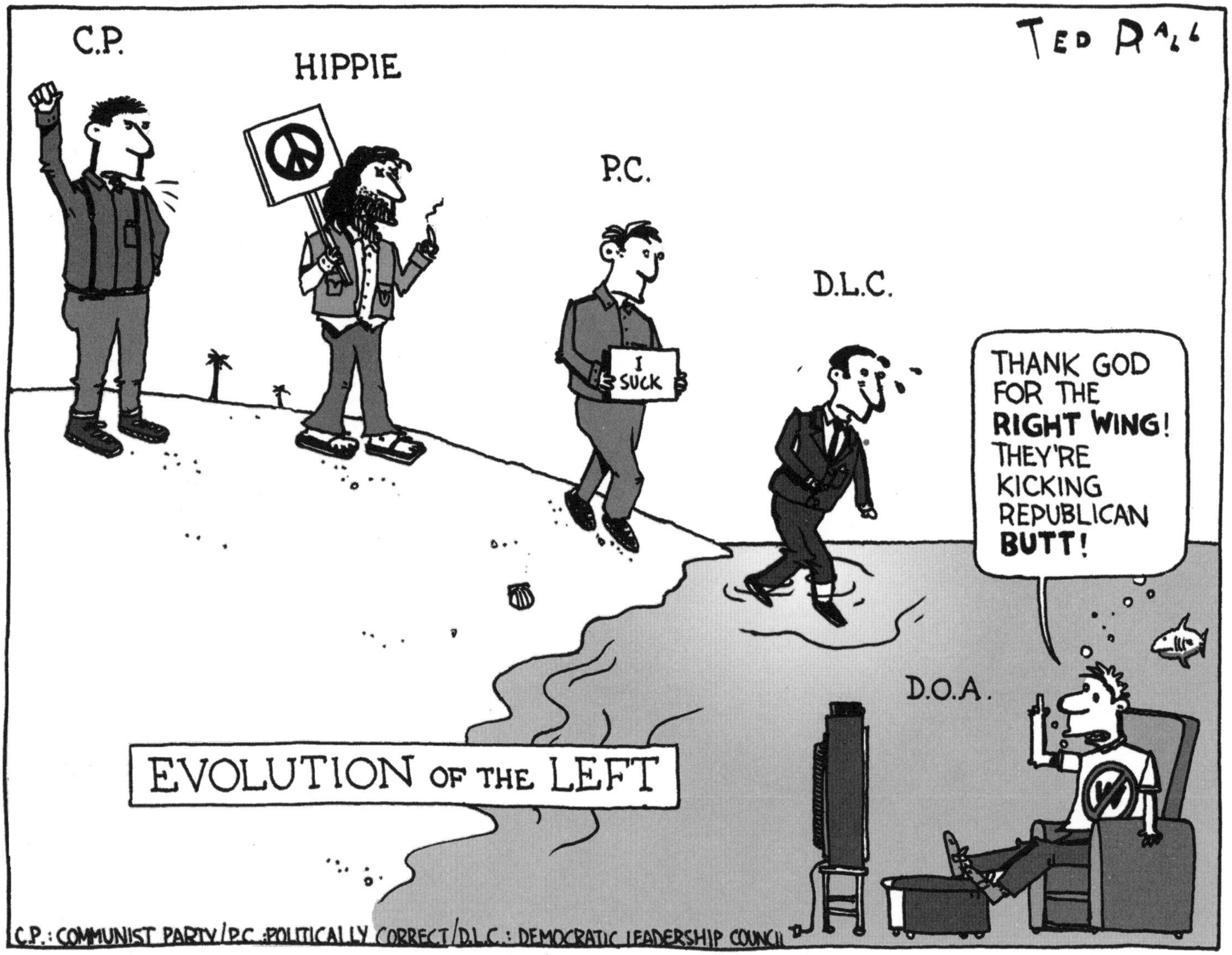
TED RALL
C.P.
HIPPIE
P.C.
I SUCK
D.L.C.
THANK GOD FOR THE RIGHT WING! THEY'RE KICKING REPUBLICAN BUTT!
D.O.A.
EVOLUTION OF THE LEFT
C.P.: COMMUNIST PARTY/P.C.:POLITICALLY CORRECT/D.L.C.: DEMOCRATIC LEADERSHIP COUNCIL

A look at what those who capture American troops in the Middle East might think about U.S. public opinion.

"Intelligent Design" posits that the universe functions perfectly, proving God's existence.
What are this theory's proponents seeing that I can't?

A revision of the famous Martin Niemöller quote about apathy among non-Jews during World War II.

YOU CAN'T BRING THEM BACK BUT YOU **CAN** REPLACE THEM. SIGN UP FOR THE
DEAD IRAQI SUBSTITUTION PROJECT

I WAS AN ORDINARY AMERICAN: BORED, MAXED OUT AND UNDEREMPLOYED.

THEN A FRIEND TOLD ME ABOUT AMERICA'S PLEDGE TO MAKE UP FOR THE IRAQIS WE KILLED.

HI, DAVE.

"DAVE" IS NO MORE. I'M NOW MOHAMMAD HASSAN, A TRUCK DRIVER KILLED NEAR BASRA IN 2004.

COOL!

JUST 6 WEEKS OF CULTURAL BOOT CAMP, AND I WAS READY TO TAKE THE PLACE OF A DEAD IRAQI!

TELL ME YOU'RE NOT WEARING **SHOES** INSIDE!

FIX THAT, HIJAB!

BEFORE I KNEW IT I WAS IN IRAQ: A LIVING BREATHING BALL OF PENANCE.

أنا زوجتك جديدة.

غريبة.

I AM YOUR NEW WIFE.

WEIRD.

SURE, THERE WERE SOME AWKWARD MOMENTS. BUT

HA HA! ELECTRICITY WOULD MAKE THIS TV SHOW STILL FUNNIER!

خارجا! اسرعة!

SIGN UP NOW! NEW OPPORTUNITIES OPENING DAILY.

WHERE WILL I FIND ANOTHER SUBSTITUTE WIFE?!

COULD IT BE **YOU**?

Hey, if we really want to help . . .

In the "flypaper strategy" argument, proponents of war in Iraq argue that we have to fight "them" "there" to avoid having to fight "them" "here." I'm old enough to remember the same argument, in utter defiance of geography, made by those who wanted to remain in Vietnam.

The White House admitted ordering the National Security Agency to spy on members of Greenpeace and other Americans, supposedly as part of the war on terrorism.

SHIBA INUS, THE SMALL FOXY DOGS THAT BECAME TRENDY IN 1998, ONCE REIGNED SUPREME IN BIG CITIES.

THAT'S RIGHT: I'M ORNERY, COST $1,000, AND YOU HAVE TO PICK UP MY DROPPINGS, BITCH.

DOGS LIVE 13 YEARS, YET THE SHIBA INU HAS ALL BUT VANISHED. WHERE DID THEY GO?

CUTE PUGGLE! VERY HIP. WHAT HAPPENED TO YOUR SHIBA INU?

NEVER HAD ONE. GO AWAY.

THE AKITA, THE FAD BREED OF THE 1980s, ONLY LASTED A FEW YEARS. WHAT HAPPENED?

MISSI

Breed of exoti
expensive dog
supposedly de
imperial guar
Japan, these
large dogs ar
tenacious

CHILDREN HAVE BEEN TOLD NOT TO WORRY.

DID I GET RID OF MY PET AFTER HE BECAME AS EMBARRASSING A RELIC AS BOY GEORGE? NO! I DID NOT.

BETWEEN US ADULTS, HOWEVER:

TWO WORDS: SCHOOL LUNCHES.

TED RALL

TRADITIONAL CHARITIES PROVIDE TEMPORARY HELP. ONLY ONE N.G.O. ATTACKS POVERTY AND HUNGER BY EMPOWERING PEOPLE MILITARILY:

 # ORDNANCE SANS FRONTIÈRES

THIS 8-YEAR-OLD BOY, ONCE DOOMED TO HUNGER AND STARVATION IN SAHARAN AFRICA, HAS BECOME A PROFICIENT AK-47 GUNMAN.

NO MORE LINING UP WITH A BOWL FOR ME — THANKS TO ARMAMENTS WITHOUT BORDERS, MY FAMILY IS PROSPEROUS! OH, AND PLEASE SEND AMMO.

WE WILL!

DESPAIR IS ANCIENT HISTORY FOR THIS TAJIK FARMER-TURNED-STINGER MISSILE KING. AND RAYTHEON LIKES THE BUSINESS.

A PASSENGER JET! I'LL BE EATING FAT WESTERN TOURISTS FOR MONTHS!

SOME MIGHT DISAGREE WITH OUR METHODS, BUT THERE'S NO ARGUING WITH RESULTS.

GIVE A MAN A FISH AND HE'LL EAT FOR A DAY. GIVE HIM AN RPG-7 AND HE CAN TAKE OVER HIS PROVINCE!

OSF

RPG

Teach a man to blow a jet out of the sky and he eats for a decade.

Bush continued the torture of detainees despite a new law explicitly forbidding the practice.

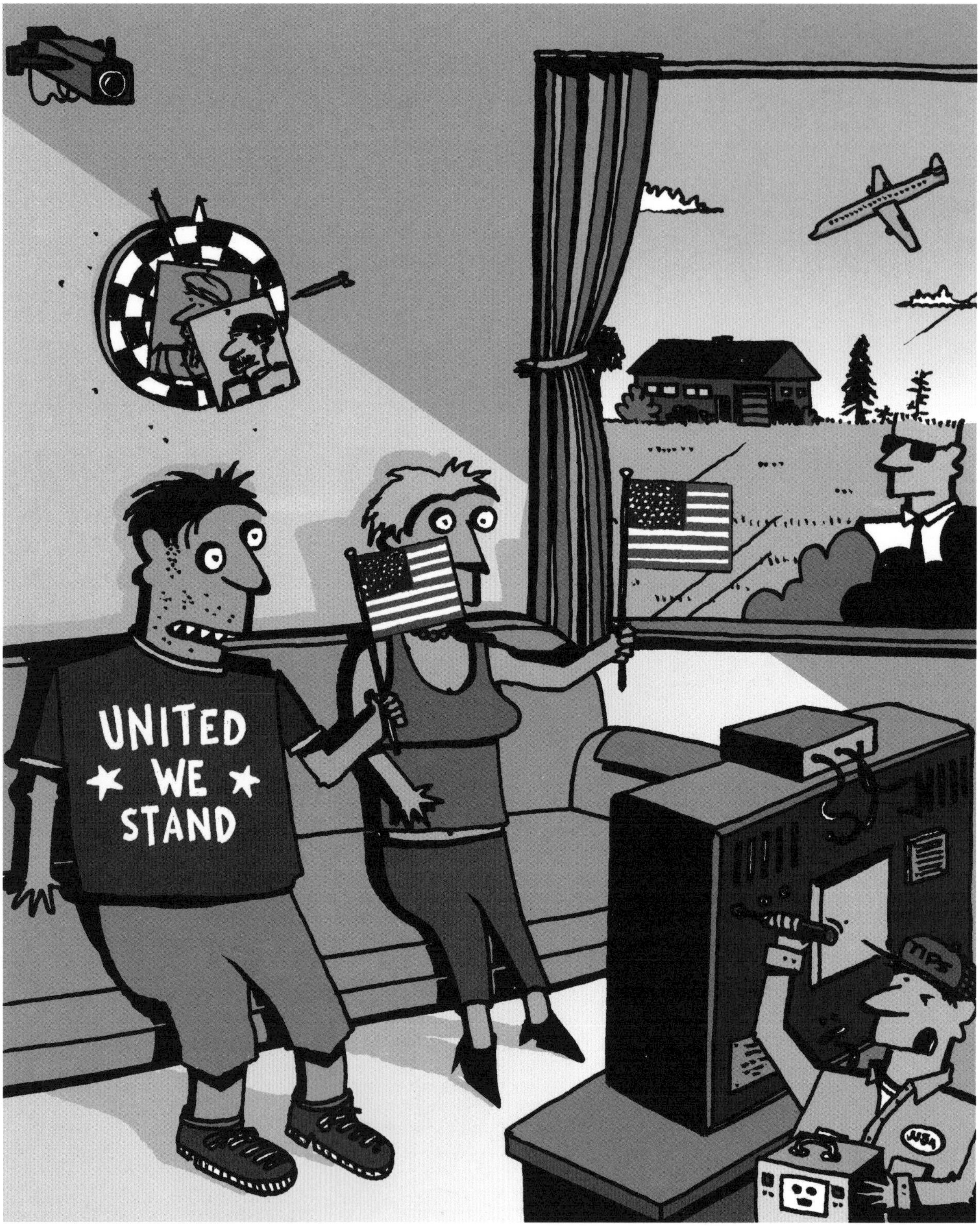
UNITED
★ WE ★
STAND